Managing restructuring

Collinson Grant

Produced and published by:

Collinson Grant
33 St James's Square
London
SW1Y 4JS

ISBN 978 0 9564337 4 9

Collinson Grant Limited

Ryecroft Aviary Road Manchester M28 2WF United Kingdom

Telephone: +44 161 703 5600
E-mail: postmaster@collinsongrant.com

Printed in the United Kingdom using paper produced from sustainable sources.
Design, typesetting and production – Centrix Q2 Limited www.cq2.co.uk

Managing restructuring

Restructuring large businesses has been at the heart of Collinson Grant's activities since the early 1980s. We have helped to get better returns from assets, to increase operating results and to improve the competitiveness of companies in the United Kingdom, in mainland Europe and in the United States. Our work as management consultants focuses on costs, organisation and people. We use this simple framework to manage complex assignments – often with an international dimension – and to support managers on smaller, more focused projects. Supporting clients in responding to changed circumstances, in seizing opportunities and in strengthening their businesses is a constant feature of our work. The notes at the back summarise what we do.

www.collinsongrant.com

Collinson Grant

Contents

Getting it right

1

Put the right executives in the right jobs at the right time

2

Have absolute clarity about the purpose of the restructuring and what it should achieve

3

If necessary, deal promptly and decisively with any cash crisis

4

Know where you are starting from – and how you will measure improvements

5

Plan meticulously but be prepared to respond quickly to the unexpected

6

Act decisively – once there is a clear path to improved performance

7

Establish accountability and matching controls

8

Confirm the new organisational structure – but only after the revised business model and improved processes are in place

1. Introduction

Restructuring – who calls the shots?

1 Introduction

Restructuring – who calls the shots?

In restructuring projects, the person who authorises substantial change influences the conduct of the whole project as well as its chances of success.

Restructuring may be on the agenda because a new or outside agent is exercising the power to shake things up with a desire to draw a new baseline for performance and a target for improvement. The opportunity may have arisen because of new owners, or after new executives have been appointed – people who have the confidence to see through real change where previously the will, energy and organisation might have been lacking.

The trigger for action is often an acquisition, a trade merger or an investment of private equity. It can also be associated with migration of authority from shareholders to creditors, such as a lender who may have swapped debt for equity.

When a new force becomes involved the power of incumbent interests, usually the managers themselves, is suddenly reduced. Then the barriers begin to fall much more readily, and the previously unthinkable suddenly becomes possible.

> ❝Willingness to change is a strength even if it means plunging a part of the company into confusion for a while.❞
>
> **Jack Welch**

This rarely happens when the established management team attempts to run a restructuring programme. In that situation it is more likely that there will be conflict as those with an interest in the status quo prepare to struggle with the advocates of change. This is the point at which skilled and determined leaders are most valuable.

This book is written from the point of view of any agent of change, who is bent on improving a business's performance and who has the necessary authority and leadership skills. In such circumstances it is common for Collinson Grant to provide support, perhaps for a new chief executive after an acquisition, a private equity investor or an exposed lender. But we also help chief executives or chief operating officers who are dissatisfied with their own organisation's performance and have the vision and ambition to initiate far-reaching improvements.

Here, success depends on those leaders and their teams of managers being able to change behaviour and be as radical as any new, external agent would be. They must be prepared to take the liberated action that an outsider would adopt. In short, executives running restructuring need to see their business in the way that potential acquirers would.

A word of warning

Restructuring is commonly thought to be the coordination of a (sometimes complex) set of processes to change the shape and effectiveness of a business organisation. It is easy for managers to see it as an internal rather than external exercise. But what is going on in the market can have much more effect on profit than the sum of many internal changes, however necessary they might be.

Getting the business in shape should be a prelude to prompt and direct action to set a target for growth and to do everything necessary to reach it. This may come about as a result of being able to serve customers better with enhanced products and more responsive service. It should also lead to a thorough examination of pricing to ensure that margins are protected and increased wherever possible. Knowing what volumes the business is likely to achieve, and at what price, informs the size, costs and design of the restructured organisation.

Phases of a project

Work on different phases can proceed in parallel, providing there is controlled scheduling. The timings shown roughly reflect the proportion of effort in each work stream. In practice it depends on the scope and scale of the project and the size of the organisation.

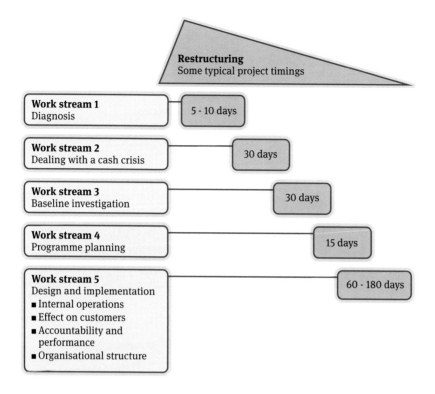

Restructuring
Some typical project timings

Work stream 1 Diagnosis	5 - 10 days
Work stream 2 Dealing with a cash crisis	30 days
Work stream 3 Baseline investigation	30 days
Work stream 4 Programme planning	15 days
Work stream 5 Design and implementation ■ Internal operations ■ Effect on customers ■ Accountability and performance ■ Organisational structure	60 - 180 days

This book describes five work streams. They can be run in sequence as phases of a single project. But the need for work streams 1 and 2, Diagnosis and Dealing with a cash crisis, will depend on the circumstances under which restructuring is contemplated. Work streams 3, 4 and 5 are the main phases of any restructuring project. Ideally, every project should be subject to investigation to establish facts and flush out the justification for change. Similarly, there must then be a plan for a programme of action, followed by its execution.

Part one

Work stream 1 – Diagnosis

All projects need a purpose, a rationale and aims. These may already be implicit because of the circumstances in which an acquisition has been made. Or something more explicit – a diagnosis – may be needed to clarify them. Careful and rational selection of objectives is the basis of all successful endeavours.

Work stream 2 – Dealing with a cash crisis

If a liquidity crisis is diagnosed, it must become the priority. The need to attend to a cash crisis before beginning the baseline investigation might already be apparent from due diligence carried out before the acquisition or may have been established immediately after taking control. Alternatively, a succession of poor results may have left the business financially unstable.

Work stream 3 – Baseline investigation

This is the systematic, though not necessarily slow, preparation that will validate the business case for restructuring and set the specific challenges for change. Prepared minds get the best results. Thorough application here will give the strongest possible indication of where the later effort to create improvements should be focused. The investigation itself should proceed briskly, but all time spent will be paid back in enhanced performance later, ultimately saving time and money.

Work stream 4 – Programme planning

Drawing up the programme of work and getting strong governance and enough people and money in place is itself a stage in the restructuring project. Quality of planning will either propel things forward or limit the quality and speed of change that follows.

Part two

Work stream 5 – Design and implementation

Later sections describe in more detail some of the tools, techniques and processes used in work stream 5, a phased programme to turn around or transform a business. The difference between these two types of restructuring is one of degree. 'Turnaround' implies modifying to improve. 'Transform' means to change by replacing processes and organisational structures and accountabilities with new ones.

Some risks and their consequences

Any programme of change has an element of risk. The eventual outcome may turn out to be very different from the original intention. Good preparation and thorough planning will minimise unexpected consequences but can never eliminate the chances of something going wrong. So it is as well to be aware at the outset of what might happen and how it could be avoided.

Most importantly, the potential effect on customers must be properly understood. Loyal and long-standing clients are the ones most likely to spot unannounced changes: they can become unsettled; they may be tempted to hedge their bets by trying other suppliers; or they may consider delaying or reducing planned orders.

New processes or upgraded systems usually do not work flawlessly first time. The consequences might be dire: late deliveries; faulty products or services; delayed or incorrect invoicing – with a knock-on effect on cash flow. The greater the planned change, the more effort should be put into understanding how it will affect customers and how any adverse effects can be mitigated. This is why many restructuring plans delay radical changes which affect customers until later in the programme of work. When the rest of the business is stable, full attention can be devoted to minimising problems.

---

66 The important thing is not to stop questioning. 99
Albert Einstein

Some changes have predictable effects; others may have unexpected consequences:

- **Controlling raised expectations** – most experienced managers know it is folly to make over-optimistic forecasts of future performance. Nevertheless, restructuring is all about improving results. Investors, other outside parties and employees need to understand how and when objectives might be met.
- **Maintaining momentum** – each restructuring exercise needs to proceed at the right pace, taking account of the circumstances the business finds itself in. Delays in certain tasks are almost inevitable for predictable or unforeseen reasons. Planning must take account of this possibility, particularly when elements of the work depend on each other.

- **Over-burdening managers** – it is reasonable to expect that managers will be under more pressure during a radical reorganisation. This can be alleviated by temporarily relieving them of some of their normal duties and asking some to concentrate on the restructuring. Conversely, it is essential to keep line managers fully involved, as they have to run the reconstructed business.
- **Losing control of the business** – it sounds dramatic but the risk is that management reporting fails to keep pace with change and generates delayed or erroneous information. The fundamentals for controlling the business are unlikely to change, but the means of measuring performance might.
- **Unsettling the staff** – many volumes have been published on the troubling effect of change. But restructuring often results in people leaving the business as a result of redundancy or fear of impending change. What is important is to avoid losing the wrong people – managers and specialists necessary for the stability of the business – who might be unsettled by what is happening and become tempted by greener pastures. This should be foreseen and tackled, perhaps by enhanced rewards.
- **Spending too much** – as we comment later, restructuring often costs more than expected, lasts longer and provokes a short-term dip in results. An investment plan should have suitable contingencies to allow for this.

A note on restructuring international businesses

Most of the elements of restructuring are common, regardless of where a business happens to be located, what markets it serves or what products it manufactures. In some jurisdictions there may be regulations or legislation that restrict managers' freedom to act or at least delay it. The most common concerns are regulations on competition and those that relate directly to restructuring, redundancies and their 'social' consequences.

Collinson Grant has restructured companies throughout Europe and in the United States. Success always demands a careful understanding of the prevailing culture and local customs and regulations. Usually this will mean that some members of the restructuring team must be from the countries affected and fluent in its language. Problems in communication will always threaten the enterprise.

Several European countries – not least France – have extensive legislation to protect workers during periods of change that is considerably more severe than that in the UK. Formal 'social plans' must be developed and agreed to mitigate the effects of redundancies as far as is possible. Although there are no 'short cuts', an experienced practitioner can save time and money by building effective relationships with the respective trades unions and understanding the local context. Regional political representatives and civil servants are surprisingly powerful.

Part One

2. Diagnosis

Early investigations may reveal something of the nature of the problem or opportunity, if not the full scale.

2 Diagnosis

Asking the right questions

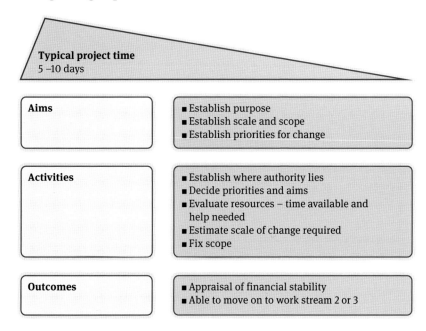

Typical project time
5 –10 days

| Aims | ■ Establish purpose
■ Establish scale and scope
■ Establish priorities for change |

| Activities | ■ Establish where authority lies
■ Decide priorities and aims
■ Evaluate resources – time available and help needed
■ Estimate scale of change required
■ Fix scope |

| Outcomes | ■ Appraisal of financial stability
■ Able to move on to work stream 2 or 3 |

Rapid initial findings may have to be combined with some judgements for which all the evidence is not yet available.

■ Who is in charge now – is there a sponsor with the necessary authority and can a team be assembled?
■ What are the priorities – what should be done first?
■ Where is the exposure – what are the present and future risks of action or inaction and how urgent is the situation?
■ What is the initial aim – and what comes after that?
■ What help do we need – have we got the skills and resources on tap and what is available immediately or on a temporary basis?

The first field of enquiry always concerns short-term financial stability. If it is fragile for, say, six months ahead, that can trigger work stream 2.

- Is liquidity a concern – can cash flow cover debts as they fall due?
- Is working capital funded adequately?
- Are banking covenants secured?

Other priorities can be diagnosed from the following questions:

- Are current profits able to sustain a healthy balance sheet?
- Is the relationship with the market or important customers secure?
- Are sales and margins slipping or stable?
- Is the quality of managers a concern or does it give confidence?
- Are budgeting, controls and information systems in place?

> *Sources of information*
> - Operating and process controls
> - Management accounts
> - Budgets
> - Statutory accounts
> - Marketing and sales forecasts
> - Customer records/satisfaction assessments/complaints
> - Managerial assessments/appraisals

Often there is a limit to the amount of time that can be spared for diagnosing problems because of the pressure to put change in hand as soon as possible. When there is time for a more orderly investigation, solutions can be sought to other common problems. These may be easier to dig out during the baseline investigation than during the initial diagnosis. But it is not wrong to examine as much as possible in the time available nor to allow initial impressions to shape thoughts on the way forward. It can be useful to develop a series of hypotheses such as:

- It seems the product range is being outsold by competitors.
- Processes and/or technology appear dated.
- Information for directors and managers looks inadequate to support strategic and/or day-to-day decisions.
- Lines of reporting seem uncertain and excessive layers of managers may be slowing down decisions and adding to costs.
- Fixed and semi-variable costs seem high in proportion to sales.
- Productivity and value for money from the payroll seem poor.

These initial impressions may change, as might priorities, but any project must start with some assumptions at the outset, if only to determine how quickly it is necessary to move towards improvement.

Purpose of restructuring

If the reasons for restructuring were not clear before diagnosis, a premise for it ought to be established at this early stage. Later, a fuller business case may confirm provisional assumptions.

A parent group, an acquirer or a new or incumbent chief executive must be sufficiently dissatisfied with the current performance of a business if changes as radical as restructuring are contemplated. But there may also be quite specific reasons beyond the desire for a business to achieve its potential, such as:

- to integrate another business following acquisition
- to align a business, following its acquisition, with the strategic direction or objectives of the new parent
- to prepare a company for sale
- to realign the business, perhaps changing its model, so that it can survive and prosper as new market challenges arise.

Scale of restructuring

Restructuring can take several forms and the amount of work needed to bring it about can vary, as the panel below indicates. For example, better management of cash and process improvements are both common elements in turnaround projects, though they may also stand alone as problems needing solutions. A transformation programme would normally incorporate the changes associated with the other three approaches.

The integration of one company with another, post-acquisition or merger, constitutes a turnaround at the least and, in extreme cases, a transformation.

Degree of change needed	**Transformation** <ul><li>Make fundamental structural change</li><li>Improve processes</li><li>Take a 3- to 6-month view</li><li>Confirm new accountabilities</li><li>Review the supply chain</li><li>Set targets for reporting</li></ul>	**Turnaround** <ul><li>Take a 45- to 90-day view</li><li>Use interim management as required</li><li>Minimise risks</li><li>Plan to reduce costs</li><li>Set new reporting standards</li><li>Implement controls over working capital and liquidity</li></ul>
Significant and business wide		
Modest and focused	**Improving processes** <ul><li>Define the problems</li><li>Use flow charting and other analyses</li><li>Implement in stages</li><li>Consider opportunities for outsourcing</li></ul>	**Cash crisis** <ul><li>Do a rapid diagnosis</li><li>Take an intensive, 30-day view to achieve results</li><li>Avoid violating debt covenants</li></ul>

3. Dealing with a cash crisis

Thankfully, this is not always a component of restructuring, but managers should know how to respond if faced with a business that is haemorrhaging cash.

3 Dealing with a cash crisis

Rapid assessment

The work stream to deal with a cash crisis is the only one where actions take precedence over planning. However, there should still be some recognisable structure and discipline in what is to be done.

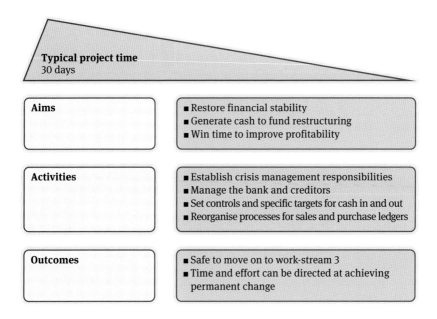

Typical project time
30 days

Aims	■ Restore financial stability ■ Generate cash to fund restructuring ■ Win time to improve profitability
Activities	■ Establish crisis management responsibilities ■ Manage the bank and creditors ■ Set controls and specific targets for cash in and out ■ Reorganise processes for sales and purchase ledgers
Outcomes	■ Safe to move on to work-stream 3 ■ Time and effort can be directed at achieving permanent change

If a company remains under the control of its incumbent managers they will not, presumably, be contemplating a general restructuring of operations while dealing with a cash flow crisis. The problems of liquidity will already have been felt and if the managers are up to the task they will already be dealing with it.

But a chief executive who has just joined after an acquisition or who is fashioning a turnaround, may face an unexpected cash crisis. In any case, a rapid assessment of the forward cash position would be routine on the first day after an acquisition.

A series of coordinated measures are needed to resolve the short-term effects of poor liquidity and shortage of working capital. Some of those referred to below might be good sense even in a 'business as usual' situation, or where an acquired business has been operating in a sub-standard way.

But where there is an actual crisis, the assumption must be that doing the right things and doing them better might not be enough. Energy and focus are the added ingredients which lead to transformation.

> *"Annual income twenty pounds, annual expenditure*
> *nineteen and six, result happiness.*
>
> *Annual income twenty pounds, annual expenditure*
> *twenty pounds ought and six, result misery."*
>
> **Charles Dickens (from David Copperfield)**

Actions

Assign responsibilities clearly and with authority

- Make it clear that a director, and a deputy, are responsible for control and for the daily and weekly actions.
- Assign subordinate responsibilities for control of debtors, creditors, cash planning, contact with the bank et cetera.
- Establish a baseline position from the beginning.
- Put in place daily (or, if less severe, weekly) reporting of cash balances and forecasts.
- Put in writing instructions and processes. Issue precise directions and train staff.

In addition to immediate actions to control payments, responsibility needs to be assigned for reducing overheads, payroll and costs generally. The conservation of cash may take precedence over the need to make sales, but this is a decision to be taken at the highest level.

Manage the bank

It is almost always the bank that ends the life of a company, so it is vital to manage this relationship. Realistically, if the bank has a policy to summarily terminate customers in trouble then there is little that can be done. Even if covenants and cash flow forecasts have been explored before an acquisition, nasty shocks can still happen. Unless the situation is dire, a lender may be prepared to throw a lifeline to a newly arrived leader, but this must be requested because it will probably not be offered.

The temptation not to reveal the whole truth to the bank should be resisted, and where possible the bank should be told of a problem well before the lowest point is reached. A constant flow of information will build more trust than intermittent figures, which would be regarded by the bank as less reliable. Those responsible need to provide the finance department with continuous information on cleared balances.

Review borrowings and act

If the cash crisis arrives after an acquisition, further funds from the investor or the parent company or group may be the best way to avoid disaster. This may not remove the need for action on cash, since the new parent or owner will still demand improvement and will want its money back.

Nevertheless a cash injection will take the pressure off and allow a more measured, and therefore more certain and efficient, improvement in the company's fortunes.

Purchase ledger, creditors and expenditure savings

This is where organisation and discipline should begin in earnest. Assume that everything 'needs tightening up'.

- Credit taken needs to be stretched. There will be some suppliers with whom the best policy is to negotiate and others whose patience can simply be tested.
- Purchase ledger staff also need to work with procurement and operations to limit purchases. It is crucial to control what is ordered when struggling to manage actual payments as they fall due.
- For control purposes the purchase ledger should be classified in relation to cash income and expenditure. Some purchases, such as raw materials for example, are necessary to support production and thus generate income. Inventories of raw materials and finished goods will need a review. Payroll needs to be paid, but redundancies may be necessary. Banks often release overdraft to pay one-off costs whilst continuing to restrict funds needed to trade. Spending on overheads can be deferred and many items cut altogether without damage to the business in the short or even the medium term.

Sales ledger and debtors

- Credit controllers need to enforce payment terms vigorously with debtors.
- Customers who depend on the business may agree to pay sooner than contracted.
- No company ever solved a cash crisis by increasing its order book and expanding the value working its way along its supply chain. On the contrary, planners should prioritise orders which are either:
  - ➤ for products and services of above average margin, or
  - ➤ for customers who pay promptly.

Centralised cash control and forecasts

Survival depends above all on exercising control from a single point of management.

- All the actions listed above should be coordinated by the head of finance or a deputy with specific responsibility for maintaining a centralised record of cash income, payments and balances, including short-term forecasts.
- Although the emphasis is on short-term liquidity to ensure survival, the medium-term cash flow forecast remains essential for recognising trends for better or worse and for taking decisions accordingly.
- Capital and other discretionary expenditure should be postponed or cancelled.
- Payment moratoriums might be sought on debt repayments, dividends and, in extreme cases, taxation.

Moving on

If the medicine is working it will first be seen in the overdraft. If it is not, the bank may inform the company that it has breached its covenants and the end will be nigh.

A steadily improving bank balance will show up on the balance sheet as a rise in net assets. But they must be the right kind of assets. For example, improving liquidity should not always end up as increases in inventory. A larger stock of finished goods may be justified if it means the business can once more afford to provide its expected standard of service to customers. But higher inventory just for 'comfort' would be no way to reap the benefits won from defeating a cash crisis. The same reasoning applies to credit given. But better liquidity can fund the working capital necessary to support increased sales.

4. Baseline investigation

A firm platform is necessary to assess progress, justify investment and confirm success. The baseline investigation starts to get under the skin of the business.

4   Baseline investigation

Why a baseline?

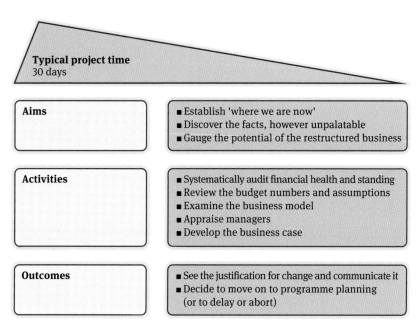

Typical project time
30 days

Aims	■ Establish 'where we are now' ■ Discover the facts, however unpalatable ■ Gauge the potential of the restructured business
Activities	■ Systematically audit financial health and standing ■ Review the budget numbers and assumptions ■ Examine the business model ■ Appraise managers ■ Develop the business case
Outcomes	■ See the justification for change and communicate it ■ Decide to move on to programme planning (or to delay or abort)

If the present is not well understood, the future is less secure and a necessary foundation for implementing change is missing. In all projects there has to be a point at which the line between the present and what comes next is drawn – a baseline.

Incumbent managers know more about their business than new managers but sometimes may understand less about markets or technology et cetera. This alone justifies a thorough baseline investigation of the business.

An acquiring organisation needs to know the condition of the business it has bought. Due diligence, carried out before the deal is completed, often provides little enough useful intelligence because it is done too quickly and because expensive specialists have not tested the business model.

This section describes an investigation that might be commissioned by a new chief executive in search of better performance by the organisation. It assumes that the initial diagnosis, described in Section 2, has been done and that a rationale for restructuring has been put forward and accepted.

Financial health

Financial stability

By now it will have been established whether there is a crisis. But even if not, the scope for better practice and improved performance needs to be investigated systematically. The first place to look is the overdraft, with particular attention to its trend and degree of fluctuation. Stability can also be measured from ratios for liquidity and gearing. Banking covenants need to be understood, the headroom quantified, and forecasts made. The general approach can mirror the actions described in the cash crisis work stream.

Debt and liquidity must be clearly understood because this might limit what the restructuring process can achieve.

Debt

Investigation will discover:
■ what does it consist of?
■ how did it originate?
■ what instruments govern it?
■ when are repayments due?
■ what banking covenants exist?
■ on what is debt secured?
■ what is the size of the bank overdraft?
■ how much interest cover is there?
■ overall, is debt in the right proportion to the rest of the balance sheet?
■ what is the strategy for managing debt?
■ how much are trade creditors owed?

Refinancing debt quickly is rarely possible and some creditors may demand to know much more about the wider plans for restructuring the business. Therefore, the first thing to do is to open dialogue in an appropriate sequence. Like all important communication, it will probably need to be conducted face-to-face to be effective.

Challenge the status quo

Restructuring is meant to break moulds. An experienced acquisitive group bought a construction materials company – an industry of which it had no previous knowledge.

Analysis of sales and margins by the acquisition team showed that profitability was determined by the cost of heavy haulage and the locations from which major customers' construction sites were served.

A combination of flexible pricing structures, closure of some locations and expansion of others, improved logistics planning and new self-billing contracts with independent hauliers broke the traditional mould of industry practice.

The success of the new business model and the restructuring that put it in place had a transformational effect. It took by surprise those managers whose service pre-dated the acquisition, many of whom were convinced that all ideas worth trying in their mature industry would have long since been adopted. This was not the case.

Liquidity

- How positive, marginal or negative is it?
- How stable and predictable is it?
- What is the quality of cash flow forecasting?
- How is cash applied – for working capital for growth, for investment in assets, for inventory?
- What is the distribution to shareholders?
- Is cash a restraint on trading and on the options for restructuring?
- How much do trade debtors owe, and is action required?

Virtually all company failures result either from being overwhelmed by debt and subsequent action by creditors, or from poor liquidity constraining working capital. If not already present, key measures should be put in place – particularly the liquidity and quick ratios.

Attention should be divided between three aspects of profit and loss.

Generation of revenue

What are the sales figures, is the revenue sustainable and from what sources is it coming? When were prices last adjusted and how is pricing regulated?

Profitability

How adequate are margins as a percentage of sales value, and are they under pressure from price or cost?

Costs

Are costs under control or on a rising trend and, if so, why? What is the basic business model which does, or should, generate profit, and is its capacity to add value being distorted for any reason? What is the trend in payroll and pay rates?

The balance sheet

Its health can easily be assessed from the answers to the following:
■ Is capital being replenished by reserves fed from profit and loss?
■ How much of the capital is owned by the shareholders and how much by lenders and creditors?
■ What has been the trend in net assets?
■ Is capital expenditure planned, how is it being financed, and is too late to review it?
■ Is the company a persistent consumer of investment capital and what is its proportion to the depreciation charge?
■ What are the authorisation processes for capital expenditure?

Control

Is the finance function under control? The trend in financial ratios and the movement in the elements of working capital – inventory, credit given and taken – need to be appraised and a balanced scorecard of performance established. Ratings are needed – satisfactory, room for improvement and poor will indicate much about what restructuring could achieve.

The budget

The value of the budget

Many consultants think that an effective way of investigating factors influencing business performance is to study the current budget and the process that created it. Budget headings provide a convenient and logical checklist for investigating what assumptions managers are currently making and what will affect their behaviour and performance. Discussions with departmental staff, as well as their managers, will be necessary if the best possible picture of strengths and weaknesses is to be obtained.

Similarly, in most organisations top managers usually contribute less to an investigation than those lower down who are closer to the actual challenges presented by the budget. The day jobs of senior managers can take them far away from the coalface and they tend to tell it how it ought to be, rather than how it is.

The results of these enquiries are usually revealing. The absence of sufficient information to form a picture, or of credible assumptions behind data, are as indicative of the general health of the managerial processes as almost anything that can be learned in other ways.

Sales and production

The investigation should ask how volumes are budgeted or forecast. Are volumes determined by the views of production managers or do sales managers take responsibility? Are sales first budgeted by volume or by value? Do sales forecasts reflect how much the company can produce or how much it is estimated that customers will buy? Is budgeted sales revenue mainly determined by prices or are average selling prices merely a statistic that falls out of the budget? What reliable analysis is there of sales by channel and market?

Complexity

Are analyses available on the mix of products, customers and channels and their relative profitability? What is the scope for rationalising product lines, simplifying processes and improving design, including the selection of materials?

Overheads

How is the need for indirect cost judged? What is it as a percentage of sales revenue? Is it clear what makes up overhead? How is overhead cost recovered in sales?

Payroll and headcount

Are employee numbers recorded in the organisation chart? What are the demographic profiles? How deep are layers of organisation and how broad are spans of control? What are average pay rates and how much overtime is worked? Is there a grade structure? How quickly does labour turn over? What is the profile of the managers and are there too many? What trends in total pay are evident?

Supply chain

How are purchase prices determined? Is there a process for testing value for money? How much is spent on transport and movement? What are the statistics for inventory? Who is responsible for inventory?

Productivity

Is productivity measured and how? Is it improving? Who has accountability?

Managerial information systems

How up to date is the IT system and what systems and software are there? Who is served by the streams of information it produces? What does it cost?

❝*Facts are stubborn things, but statistics are more pliable.*❞
Mark Twain

Locations

Is the company geographically dispersed or is it split up in other ways? Are there too many or too few locations? Why is it split up and is this essential to the business model? What does it mean for the budget process? What does it cost?

The business model

Successful organisations are good at what they do. Really successful businesses have a model that differentiates them from others, particularly others that compete with them for customers, investment, rights over technology or scarce inputs.

The differentiated parts of the model could, for example, include operating strategies, methods such as specialised design or use of otherwise generic industrial or commercial processes, or a proprietary innovation. At one time internet retailing came into this category, although it is now commonplace and overtaken by time and events.

There is little point in a general restructuring if the company is not conscious of how its model makes it competitive; why it is winning or failing to do so; and how restructuring would strengthen its position. A model has several dimensions of which the first two are most important: policy made up of deliberate choices; and strategy that determines how it operates.

Policy versus strategy

The following example of one real business in private ownership differentiates policy from strategy.

The business policy

Policy is about what a business wants to be and wants to do.

- Chosen market sector – engineering fastenings.
- Position in supply chain – wholesale distribution.
- Type and amount of return sought by controlling shareholders –between 12 and 16 per cent on capital employed.
- Development – continuing family ownership, fast growth not essential.

The business strategy

Strategy is how the policy is being pursued operationally. For example including:

- using chosen channels for market and sales organisation (eg, direct sales representation)
- product range and pricing
- an outbound UK call centre, targeting specific margins and mix
- sourcing (Far East, 60 per cent from three unrelated suppliers)
- inventory (UK bulk store, stock turn not less than 5)
- operations (self-managed, break-bulk packaging)
- logistics (contract outbound carriage).

A stitch in time

The properties of a business model and the processes that support it never endure forever. The solution is to recognise the risk and move on, even if the time to do so never seems right.

A printer of posters and banners did 80 per cent of its business with a nationwide chain of 250 retail stores. Its skill at delivering the right signs to the right stores just before they were needed for promotions enabled it to rebid and retain the contract for many years.

But the customer had an aging business model, got into choppy water, and failed. Although this was not entirely unexpected, it caught the printer by surprise. It was too late to transform the business and it followed its customer into oblivion.

Internal operations

Processes

Internal change is about all the operational processes, not about the effect on customers. These processes include the supply chain, transformation into product or creation of service, and the supporting functions that administer and manage the organisation itself.

The processes that are most usually associated with restructuring are those that are core to the business model. That is to say they add value that flows more or less directly into a main stream of revenue to produce profit.

Obvious examples are any processes that transform the product or deliver the service, including those that are logistical or creative, such as engineering and design. The baseline investigation needs to consider how relevant, economic or efficient the current design process is, and whether the business has been left behind by technology and changes in the best way of doing things. The investigation should be framed as an intellectual audit and include brainstorming sessions to question the status quo.

Accountability and business reporting

It is an accepted principle that all processes in a business organisation must have a responsible manager who is held accountable for performance. But even when this is taken for granted, often there are still substantial gaps in accountability.

It is also generally acknowledged that accountability is judged by measuring performance. It follows that if performance cannot be quantified and reported there is something wrong with the design of the process for which the manager is responsible, in the way that it is being managed, or with the information used to measure it. One of the purposes of the baseline investigation is to discover whether the restructuring programme should tackle any of these problems. The adequacy of the IT systems infrastructure should not be overlooked.

Control requires that there be a sound basis for reporting the business. The means of control include the dashboard of information that measures managers' achievements against expectation, detects the need to improve performance by revealing variances, and reports business results with sufficient analysis to inform decisions.

Organisational structure

There needs to be a consistent logic about the way managerial accountability fits together in the structure of the organisation. The depth of the layers in line reporting and the width of the spans reporting into managers have strong implications for the number of employees, payroll cost, and how flexible operations are. A business that is slow and inflexible in its responses to customers, or struggles with the flow of information between its parts, may find a solution in changing its structure.

There is great potential for reconfiguration, even if nothing else in the business changes. But if there is a change in processes or other aspects of the business, the shape of the organisation must also be modified.

Act in haste...

Not all the most important employees are top managers. One company in the haulage industry acquired another. Within days an acrimonious exchange resulted in an elderly traffic clerk being discharged.

It quickly became apparent that this person had the only record, held in her head, of the lynchpin of the business model – the personal contacts for winning return loads.

The economics of the business were severely threatened. Incentives and entreaties for the employee to return were to no avail. Hard words could not be unspoken and the investment failed to prosper.

The effect on customers

Many restructuring programmes do not disturb the way customers are dealt with. Instead they concentrate on the economy, efficiency and effectiveness of the internal processes that create what the business sells. Improving how it takes its products and services to market, to whom it sells and how much profit is made may be of equal or greater importance, however.

It is difficult and risky to change internal and external processes at the same time. The greatest risk is in losing the confidence of customers. Many business models have important features that need to be handled with care. For example, the business may be symbiotically dependent on relationships with one or more suppliers or customers. If this is ignored or not understood by managers, or by post-acquisition investigators, then not only are margins at risk but the aims of restructuring may be misdirected. Intervention should reinforce aspects of the business that work well, not put them at risk.

This is not confined to the more obvious cases found in manufacturing. For example, in the financial services sector, an outsourced business handling insurance claims exists on a long and complicated value chain alongside the retail customers buying insurance, underwriters, brokers, outsourced call centres and the insurance company itself. All those businesses are linked through multiple inter-dependencies, mutual obligations and revenue flows. The volume of sales can be influenced through one relationship, even though the actual revenue comes from another source.

All aspects of the business model come together in recognition of where competitive advantage is to be found. All businesses survive for a reason. Some of them live for years in happy ignorance of why. A second-generation business may be owned or managed by people who never learned what its founder knew about creating competitive advantage. They may know it and think it remains unchanged, but in fact the market has moved on.

The business world learned some time ago (from Michael Porter) about three broad and very generic types of advantage around which a competitive business model can be built: the low cost producer (scale and efficiency); the differentiated product or process (new technology or scarce resources); or a uniquely valuable focus on one or a group of customers (such as an outsourcing service operator might build).

❝ Drive thy business or it will drive thee. ❞
Benjamin Franklin

A prospective acquirer could position its desired takeover target within Porter's spectrum of competitive advantage and this may even be the reason for the acquisition. But a lot of the detail about how the whole model operates may not be understood until the post-acquisition investigator gets at close quarters with the processes, systems and other aspects of how the whole model works.

Assessing the business model

Some symptoms of a model that may be out of its time are:

- declining trends in profitability (absolute level of profit might be satisfactory)
- growth slower than competitors, or lack of growth
- migration of customers
- poor record of introducing new products
- loss of a channel to market (for whatever reason)
- difficulty with recruitment into important posts or with senior managerial succession
- not reinvesting the depreciation charge or at a lower rate than competitors
- conflicts with industry regulators.

Some of these symptoms may be apparent to a prospective acquirer, others may be awaiting discovery. An incumbent manager (or consultant) may even spot the risk. Any such assessment should draw a business in the direction of restructuring.

Getting the business model right

Hanson plc was expert at acquisition and bought many companies with good but under-worked assets. After an acquisition, the new leadership always instructed incumbent middle managers to focus on achieving current budgets.

The new leadership team then set to work rethinking the business model from first principles. Thorough market research was carried out, but operational and commercial innovations that would differentiate the acquired business from its competitors were most sought after.

The restructuring always placed emphasis on systems to control cost and margin. Only when these had been designed were managers inducted into new processes, and targets for performance raised in the budget for the following year.

The baseline investigation should include the general market and economic prospects for the business. Particular attention should be given to listening to the customers. It is in their hands whether there is a good or bad time ahead. However, their views and those of the managers should be received with caution by a post-acquisition team.

Thinking ahead

In the acquisition of a large supplier of construction materials the incoming team asked the incumbents what preparation had been made for the forthcoming downturn in the industry. The response was: 'what downturn?' Shortly thereafter began the worst construction recession the industry had suffered for twenty years. By the time it gathered pace the more sceptical and prescient new management team was well advanced in its preparations, reducing the size of its business ahead of its competitors.

Opportunities to reduce cost

It is rare for any programme of change to exclude the aim of making savings. This is as it should be. In addition to all the other good reasons for spending less to achieve the same or more, savings help to pay for restructuring programmes, which can be expensive.

As soon as plans are being laid to undertake a programme of change, requests to reduce cost appear like magic out of the woodwork. Sponsors begin to talk about 'quick wins' and 'low hanging fruit'. But cynicism about easy change and easy money is pointless. Project sponsors always want some promises, so the baseline investigation should include some brainstorming as a way to flush out ideas.

Management

Need for a shake-up

Successful restructuring depends more than anything else on appointing the right executives to the senior jobs in the company. Otherwise it will be too risky to make the degree of change required. Restructuring depends entirely on senior executives becoming fully involved in the task. If they cannot, then the best option may be to abort.

> **❝*Never go to excess, but let moderation be your guide.*❞**
> **Cicero**

It is prudent to expect that in a shake-up not all the senior managers will survive. But it is always the case that those who do not and cannot fit must be replaced sooner or later if a restructuring programme is to be successful. Inertia in all its forms and from any source is incompatible with change. Casualties should be treated humanely and generously. Those that remain will take note.

Assessing managers

Directors and senior managers in an acquired business may or may not have backgrounds and attitudes suited to a change of direction and culture. The baseline investigation needs to test their strengths and weaknesses.

There will be the temptation to form views too early of how they might fit into the restructured business or the part they should play in implementing change. Early steps may need to be taken to secure the continued services of special talent. And yet it may be worse to delay making appointments, even at the expense of a few mistakes with a few good people unnecessarily lost. Personal histories have to be understood and past failures and achievements laid bare and corroborated wherever possible.

Assessing suitability

Those leading the baseline investigation should not shy away from making judgements about people if managerial teams are to be well balanced and ready for the challenge ahead.

- Attitude to change – if the company is to commit to radical change there is no place in an important function for anyone not prepared to board the train when it departs. Change is difficult enough without unwilling passengers, whose options are a sideways move or departure from the business.
- Up to the job – capabilities have to match the future not the past. Some good people reach a level beyond which they cannot operate effectively because of their intellect, absence of up-to-date skills, or patterns of thought not appropriate to the size or complexity of their function.

- Good, but not a team player – there are often square holes for square pegs in organisations, but the question to be asked is whether the individual is likely to reduce the effectiveness of other players.
- Leadership – all senior managers have others they must lead, particularly in times of change, and those not able to do so may need to be moved into jobs requiring only specialist skills.
- Ambition – not necessarily for themselves, but they must have a desire for the organisation to succeed.
- Supportive – no chief executive should want to stifle debates on policy and strategy, but at some point managers must be supportive. Vexatious dissent cannot be tolerated once the course is set.

Modifying the managerial profile

There are a number of questions to be asked:

- Are there too many managers?
- What are the gaps in the senior management team and might these be filled by internal or external candidates?
- Who is unlikely to fit in the new organisation and how quickly should they leave?
- How much will the departures cost?
- How can other senior executives be secured and what should they be paid?
- Is there a risk of good managers leaving and how can they be retained or replaced?

Some senior managers in an acquired business will continue to exercise considerable influence and power. Are they allies or opponents of change?

The business case

The decision

The outcome of the baseline investigation should be the decision on the scope and scale of the restructuring to be attempted. Financial analysis, the health of the business model, the effectiveness of internal and external processes, and the quality of the managerial team will all indicate how the decision should go.

For many new owners or top executives of an acquired business the die will already have been cast when the bid was made. Restructuring will follow acquisition so that the business can be run 'our way'. In other circumstances there may be a case to prove. But no restructuring project should be authorised unless a business case has demonstrated the inputs, outputs, schedule of changes to be put into effect, the resources, the timetable, and the financial and operational benefits. It is not the purpose here, however, to describe how a business case for change should be prepared.

But the case will lie, overwhelmingly, in the current financial performance of the business, whether expectations are being realised and the improvement that can be achieved.

There will be quantitative and qualitative arguments to support the case, but to engage senior managers and generate the necessary sense of urgency these will have to be set out eloquently, even if most managers have no vote on the matter. All managers need to see the strength of the case and the vision of the future for which they will be expected to strive, and perhaps be rewarded.

Establishing the case

The argument for action should answer a number of questions about the proposed project, and will include:

- How is the project to be defined – its scope, aims, location etc?
- What are the specific, predicted benefits?
- How do these contribute to the overall strategy?
- What will be the cost in revenue and capital expenditure?
- How soon will the benefits be realised?
- What does success depend upon?
- Can a financial model of the proposed solution be constructed with 'what if' scenarios?
- What managerial and other employees will be needed?
- How will current operations be affected?
- What external help will be needed?
- Does the project overlap with, or contribute to, other initiatives?
- Are there opportunities for introducing best practice or benchmarking?

Finally, it needs to be borne in mind that not all problems can be solved or opportunities realised with a single project in which multiple work streams cover all perceived shortcomings. Complexity needs managing with common sense. Restructuring can fail because of too much ambition as well as too little competence.

Formulating strategy

A lot of restructuring is driven by an imperative to reduce costs. But cost is not always the primary objective. Adapting to changes in markets, improving service to customers, challenging competitors, and demonstrating a willingness to grow the investors' capital are all equally good aspirations for a restructuring programme.

A vision of where the business will be, what it will look like, and how it should behave in the future can be developed out of the case for change. This should be formulated in a series of short, unambiguous statements that set out clearly what has to be achieved and by when. These should set out the main business arguments and competitive reasoning that justify a programme of major change. This will be set out as a strategy which describes the aims of the programme and relates strongly to the business model and policy.

"There are risks to a programme of action.
But they are far less than the long-range risks
and costs of comfortable inaction."

John F Kennedy

---

5. Programme planning

Who said it? To fail to plan is to... Some say it goes back to at least the Punic Wars and is equally valid now!

5   Programme planning

Making a start

It is often assumed that there is never a right time to commence a restructuring project. But in truth it rarely matters when a start is made. More important is that the programme allows enough time to complete the job properly. Most projects start too late to succeed in meeting deadlines, leave too many tasks uncompleted and aspects of the business case unfulfilled.

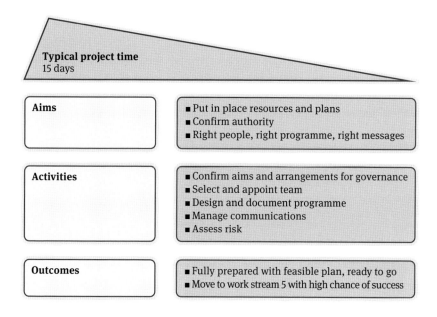

Typical project time
15 days

| Aims | ■ Put in place resources and plans
■ Confirm authority
■ Right people, right programme, right messages |

| Activities | ■ Confirm aims and arrangements for governance
■ Select and appoint team
■ Design and document programme
■ Manage communications
■ Assess risk |

| Outcomes | ■ Fully prepared with feasible plan, ready to go
■ Move to work stream 5 with high chance of success |

The essential elements of planning are:

- to confirm the aims
- to select and appoint the team
- to design and document the programme
- to decide on the timetable
- to communicate
- to consider short-term actions, risks, hidden costs and culture.

The aims

The project's aims were described in the first step of the baseline investigation. They will have been restated with any amendments in the business case. The documentation for the restructuring programme will confirm them. It is hardly possible to repeat them too often. People working on the project should be encouraged to ask at every opportunity – how will this achieve the aims?

Project team

The conventions for managing business projects are well known to all who have taken part in them (in this generation that must include most managers). That is not to say that project management and programming is always done well. Before the programme is planned, ask whether the company has the right quality and number of people, willing and committed leaders, experienced programme managers and competent team members.

Sponsor

The identity of the sponsor is critical. This task is rarely set up or performed well enough to guarantee success. The sponsor must:

- be appointed by and have the confidence of someone senior such as the chairman or chief executive, or a director, or hold one of these posts themselves
- authorise spending, including on external support
- define the purpose of the project
- issue the aims, at least in draft for confirmation in more detail by the steering group, which the sponsor will lead
- specify reporting requirements including milestones and intervals
- appoint a programme manager
- approve the project team
- indicate the acceptable length of the project
- nominate a steering group
- assess the apparent risks and benefits and give the signal to start
- control the project as a priority task, not an optional extra
- accept responsibility for the outcome.

> **"** *Change is not made without inconvenience,*
> *even from worse to better.* **"**
> **Samuel Johnson**

A common reason for failure is weak or disinterested sponsorship. If the responsibilities listed above are not properly discharged it is like entering a lame horse in the Grand National: even if it doesn't fall at Becher's Brook it will never finish the race.

Steering group

The composition of steering groups should include the most senior people, usually those heading the main departments and functions of the business. If operational processes will change as a result of the project, success will depend on the chief operating officer, or person of similar rank, attending steering group meetings either to agree proposals or to challenge them if they are flawed.

Programme manager

The third important player is the programme manager or team leader. Experience, commitment, energy, leadership skills and all round suitability is all that is required! This means that they should:

- know the business well and understand its culture
- have strong interpersonal skills and the credibility to be able to intervene quickly when the situation demands
- have a reputation as somebody who gets things done.

Restructuring projects are desperately hard work. They are shot through with many pitfalls. One of the most difficult is managing the politics. Professional project skills such as a Prince 2 qualification may be important if the scope and scale of restructuring is large.

Restructuring after an acquisition should be led by a programme manager who should, if possible, be a new senior executive reporting to the board of a parent company. They have no 'baggage', and can be relied on to propose or accept any change that has merit, however radical. Incumbent managers have more difficulty because of past associations with ideas, or with alliances and loyalties to people. Motives, real or imagined, tend to come into play.

Solve the right problem

A company engaged in industrial fastenings operated a business model in which it sourced manufactured product in China, broke bulk, packed and distributed to the wholesale trades in a number of industries. It added value but knew little about the needs of the end users, unlike the specialist wholesalers who were its customers.

It tackled the problem of falling profits by restructuring its operations: – outsourcing physical distribution, rationalising the depot structure, investing in more efficient storage to reduce inventory and speed of picking and despatch. None of this had the desired effect. The wholesalers had control over the prices paid by end users, the part of the value chain where the fattest margins were to be earned. It was the company's business model that was broken.

The main tasks of a programme manager should be:

- to confirm the strategy for change with the sponsor
- to take responsibility for planning the whole restructuring programme, select and organise the staff and provide appropriate training and briefing
- to establish and take responsibility for the processes for managing projects and restructuring, including a programme management office (PMO) which he or she may or may not run personally (depending on the scale and scope of the project)
- to control communication
- to monitor the close integration of the change programme with day-to-day plans for the business
- to assess the risks inherent in taking action and ensure that projected performance is not jeopardised. This inevitably entails balancing pragmatic short-term action with the longer-term plans for change and carrying out risk assessments.

It is also important that the programme manager should:

- apply rigorous control to the project management process, ensuring, in particular, that projects do not pass 'gates' without approval from a lead body, such as a steering group
- get senior managers to release employees from other work to ensure project teams have the right people

- conduct formal reviews of progress and issue progress reports as agreed with the steering group
- work with line managers to create and manage a process for the formal evaluation of each work stream or subset of the project.

As well as formal processes, project management needs to change behaviour, knowledge, skills and attitudes. Programme managers need to instil an ability to react more quickly to competitors. There should be no need for formal projects and external support to bring about tactical improvements.

Team members

Members of the project team dedicate some or all of their time to the project. They are often a mixture of people arriving as part of an acquisition team, current managers seconded from a day job, and external consultants. The preferred insiders are middle-ranking managers whose career paths are not yet set in stone. This is important because the more senior and more settled the manager in a department or function, the harder it is for him or her to be objective.

Careers can be enhanced by successfully leading projects. Reputations can be made. But people in senior positions have a natural conservatism which curbs innovation. The project will add little to their already well-advanced careers.

The influence of outsiders is often vital. They bring independence, objectivity and freedom from fear of change. They usually have skills and experience of direct relevance and cost nothing to let go when all is concluded. They are frequently the yeast that leavens the loaf.

If restructuring is organic – self-inflicted by the company's managers themselves – then one senior executive must fulfil the role of sponsor. Nonetheless, the programme manager always needs protection from a centre of power.

The team that will take the integration and restructuring forward should have previous experience of change and possess relevant skills. Usually it will include a small number of functional specialists and consultants with change-management experience, who may have been involved in the investigations and assessments just concluded.

Once integration is under way, tasks can be sub-divided and delegated to smaller teams with responsibility for specific outcomes. These often benefit from including line managers, either continuing in post or fully seconded.

Line managers

Some line managers may not be members of the project team, but those whose processes are to be restructured to any degree are clearly vital players in the project.

They must be involved at every stage of planning and communications as it affects their people and processes. They must be responsible for, and committed to, achieving the project's aims.

Project programme

Planning

The planning process should describe, in outline at least, the main stages of the programme, and the length of time that it ought to take. Variables include: the scope and scale of probable change, nature of the changes, locations and other logistical aspects, the resources available, deadlines imposed (usually by unreasonable sponsors), and the degrees of improvement sought.

The programme of work follows the four main parts of the baseline investigation:

> **Restructuring internal operations and processes**
> **Improving processes which affect customers**
> **Managerial accountabilities and performance**
> **Designing the organisational structure**

An experienced programme manager has the skills to schedule the timetable, dependencies and resources, and to use these to create efficient and effective work streams for the team. Tools and techniques for each part of the programme are described in Part Two.

It is not unusual for a number of people to leave the business as a consequence of restructured operations. If the numbers are substantial, careful thought needs to be given to the timing and sequencing of events, as well as the costs. The plan must reflect the legal framework for periods of notice and consultation to avoid claims for unfair dismissal. The possible impact on those remaining in the business should be considered. If some of the employees are based abroad, this can become a much more complex and time-consuming exercise.

Linking processes, accountability and organisational structure

The principal task in planning any restructuring, after an acquisition or not, is to create a plan with a logical sequence of how processes are designed and how accountability for their performance is established, with an organisational structure that suits both.

This is illustrated below. In practice the steps will be repeated until the design of processes, accountability for their performance, and the structure in which managers and business units are put, all achieve harmony.

> **"***A wrong decision isn't forever; it can always be reversed. The losses from a delayed decision are forever; they can never be retrieved.***"**
> **J K Galbraith**

Processes need to be designed so they can be measured, thus ensuring accountability for performance. The structure into which managers are put must be capable of controlling processes, and their performance measured in turn. Performance reporting must indicate how managers are fulfilling their accountabilities, whilst also measuring the productivity of processes.

The touchstone for each aspect of organisational design is how it contributes to realising the operational strategy. Both new and existing business models can be audited through these checks. Many businesses have managers and processes that are not measured, processes without responsible managers, and structures in which some managers have no defined accountabilities.

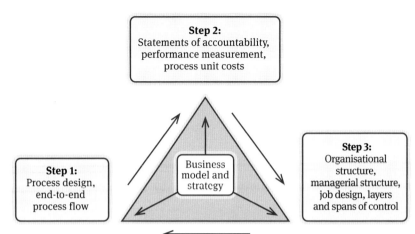

There are two dimensions to planning organisational structures:

- **Managerial structure**: how managers and employees are organised into departments; how individual accountabilities are set, jobs designed, and lines of reporting configured.
- **Business structure**: the configuration of and relationships between business units, such as intra-trading and profit centre structures.

Any change to either structure that is highlighted by the baseline investigation must be incorporated into the plan.

Selecting priorities

Planning requires selecting priorities for improvement. The restructuring team will need to prioritise and sequence each targeted activity. To do this, it may be helpful to consider:

- Which tasks will produce most benefit?
- Are the costs of change in line with the benefits, or is there a conflict?
- How does each element of the plan for change contribute to fulfilling the business case for restructuring?
- How soon can the benefits be banked?
- What will be the impact on current operations?
- Do the priority tasks overlap with, or contribute to, others that are subsidiary or incidental?

Hard and soft change

Most changes to processes have 'hard' and 'soft' aspects, both of which have to be managed. A major error is to plan time and resources for hard change, forgetting soft change altogether. Soft change nearly always takes longer, requires more skill and carries more risk of failure.

This is illustrated below:

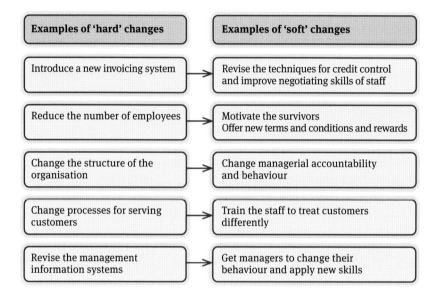

Examples of 'hard' changes	Examples of 'soft' changes
Introduce a new invoicing system	Revise the techniques for credit control and improve negotiating skills of staff
Reduce the number of employees	Motivate the survivors Offer new terms and conditions and rewards
Change the structure of the organisation	Change managerial accountability and behaviour
Change processes for serving customers	Train the staff to treat customers differently
Revise the management information systems	Get managers to change their behaviour and apply new skills

Communications

The programme needs to be explicit about the content and timetable for communication to all parts of the company. That includes telling employees if the ways they work, the structures they work in, or their jobs and terms and conditions will be affected. Changes likely to affect sites and the number of employees may give rise to multiple meetings and negotiations.

It is often overlooked that some changes to processes, particularly those that are commercial or relate to new technology, have to be communicated on a 'need to know' basis. Sometimes the principal effects of restructuring are confined to managers, for example changes to the way lines of reporting are structured, performance is measured or information technology used.

A checklist should include the following:

- Confirm the personal responsibility for all communications
- Convey consistent, simple, accurate and timely messages
- Let managers know what is going on as quickly as possible
- If it is 'business as usual', get that message out to prevent false expectations of change
- Communicate directly with people rather than put notices up
- Consider organising a management conference
- Listen for false rumours and act quickly to stop them spreading
- Communicate only as much as the degree of change demands
- Arrange to get informal reaction to communications

The success of communication is measured by the response from employees. They will respond best to propositions like a clear business plan, sensitively targeted messages to different ranks of employees, and careful timing. All those affected by an acquisition, whether inside or outside the business, must receive information that is consistent if not necessarily as complete or detailed as that given to others.

The chief executive should pause before delegating responsibility completely to another manager, for example the HR Director. The consequences of what is to be communicated will lie with him or her, so ultimate responsibility for getting the message and the medium right should also reside there.

Say what you mean

Asked what he would do if he ran China, Confucius replied: 'I would make people use language correctly. For if what is said is not meant, what should be done remains undone. And people will stand around in hopeless confusion.'

Good advice. Too many managers assert they do not have time for brevity and clarity in the written and spoken word. Yet communicating decisions is what gives meaning to their jobs.

Short-term actions

Restructuring takes time, too much for some chief executives or project sponsors. This results in pressure to achieve benefits quickly, particularly cost savings.

Managers responsible for restructuring programmes hate directives from above calling for quick results. These can distract them from other tasks which, although more time consuming, will have many times more impact.

Those directing the programme of change need to decide whether the restructuring team should have responsibility for easily-achieved cost savings. If they do, it creates a programme in two parts, with two rates of progress to manage. Alternatively, a separate team might be instructed to cut jobs, review overheads and close sites.

To judge which is the best approach the full context has to be understood. Care should be taken before splitting the responsibilities of the two programmes, whether they run concurrently or serially. It is probably better to have a single programme with priorities ordered as appropriate.

Unless sales and profit are on a clear rising trend it is rarely a mistake to cut capacity and costs, particularly overheads, and then to make assets work harder, increasing productivity with reduced unit costs. Restored profitability, followed by expansion when appropriate, will enrich margins and profits in a way not obtainable by other methods.

Short-term cuts in costs should not be allowed to delay plans for the longer-term aims of restructuring. Strategic changes to the business model should be seen as complementary to any short-term plan.

Hidden costs

From the outset the planning team should be mindful of the hidden costs the restructuring programme itself may cause, particularly if done after an acquisition. The business case should have allowed for this, although sometimes it takes the detailed programme to expose the size and shape of the trough in the diagram overleaf. The information should be used to manage expectations.

Six stages in the life of a new venture:
Enthusiasm
Sobriety
Panic
Search for guilty parties
Punishment of the innocent
Reward for those who did nothing

Before an acquisition, the performance of a target company may dip if it is known to be for sale. This disturbing effect is difficult to counter and usually worsens as the deal is completed and ownership of the business is transferred. Many acquisition plans have failed to take full account of this. Subsequent 'improvements' may go on to make the losses worse because managers are distracted by changes.

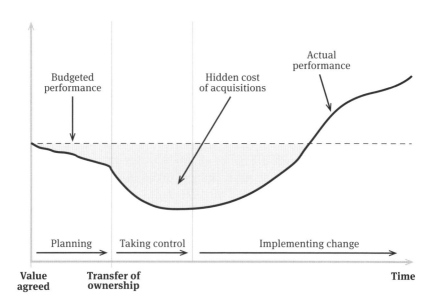

Psychology of change

Culture

Before we leave planning and move on to designing and implementing change, it is important to consider how to manage people at a time of change. Culture comprises attitudes, personal styles and expectations found in a group. This is important in business because culture always wins out over structure. It is doubly important at a time of change because structure affects efficiency and effectiveness, and therefore profit. So culture, and the psychological basis for it, is a legitimate subject for study in the context of restructuring.

Leadership

The most powerful influence on the culture of the whole organisation is leadership style. The way the top team works with the chief executive will be registered and replicated at all levels in the organisation. For example, a collegiate team at ease with itself will find, over time, similar relationships breaking out among their subordinates. But a forceful, autocratic leader with a 'tell' rather than 'ask' style will spawn similar behaviour up and down the organisation. This can work to propel an organisation forward, sometimes quickly and successfully. The risk is that the direction or scale of movement may not have been fully discussed with others or put to proper test. It is also a bet on the judgement of one person.

Managers

Managers and employees breathe in the prevailing culture. For example, the intellect that goes into defining the aims of a project is not the only criterion, the quality with which they are communicated counts in equal measure. A style that seeks to ensure people understand first, then do, is generally more effective than one in which they are expected to 'just do'. When understanding gets a hold, people are halfway to acceptance and this makes them quicker and better at achieving.

Employees

Behaviour in groups is most influenced by culture. Each business has unique cultural norms. Prevailing culture will either support or block the preparation of plans for changing the order of things and will therefore expedite or stand in the way of their fulfilment.

A creative debate about the case for change needs to be followed by firm conclusions after a decision has been made. The purpose of analysing and understanding cultural differences is to ensure that they will not prevent people from doing what is required.

Effective briefings
An experienced acquirer of companies put up no notices and issued no newsletters about change. Yet all managers and workers got all the information they needed.

Managers held need-to-know information meetings with specially assembled audiences. For example, the Finance Director called all his reports from around the country. They went back and repeated the message at one and two levels down. Soon 5,000 employees at 50 plants nationwide were fully briefed. Then everyone got on with it.

It is best to bring people together face-to-face at the planning stage. For managers, a conference as soon as the plan has been released often works well. The most disruptive factor can be an undeclared plan.

- Reduce anxiety – be open about the reasons for change, particularly after an acquisition, and say clearly if job losses are possible and when that will be known.
- Provide information rapidly – keep promises about informing people, even when the amount of information available is unavoidably limited.
- Minimise managerial 'power plays' – managers come under close scrutiny during periods of significant change and it is their behaviour that sets the tone.
- Focus action on the future – concentrate people's energy on improvement projects and the new market and other repositioning of the business, rather than dwelling on negative factors.

Reviewing progress of the plan

If progress is marked by milestones based on priorities, those priorities may suddenly or gradually shift and progress may falter.

At some point, after a series of routine progress reports, a final review becomes due. Few companies enjoy comparing the results of projects against forecasts. Things rarely go absolutely according to plan. Keeping track of something that may have taken on a life of its own may seem unnecessary but it still makes sense to compare actual outcomes with what was planned.

A continuous formal audit of progress is advised. This ensures that the performance of the investment is kept under the spotlight and, importantly, that there is an opportunity to amend or update the plan and the individual changes and improvements within it.

66*Our life is frittered away by detail...*
*Simplify, simplify.*99
Henry David Thoreau

Getting it right

It is hard to lead organisational change and secure tangible benefits. It is possible to become distracted, especially by the need to manage the business. When things start to go wrong, symptoms can include the following:

- Tasks take more time than expected
- 'Culture' is blamed when unexpected problems arise
- Other activities distract attention
- Restructuring costs increase sharply
- Skills, abilities and leadership are inadequate
- There is insufficient attention to detail
- Inadequate training and support are available
- External factors affect progress adversely
- The implementation is neither accurately defined nor monitored carefully

By motivating people, it is possible to prevent or cope with these ill-effects. It is essential to show confidence in the managers who implement innovation, take unpopular decisions, operate new processes and have precise targets which are tightly monitored.

Despite the best planning, the latest technology and fully committed directors, success depends largely on the energy, enthusiasm and skills of middle managers – 'the marzipan layer' below the icing and above the cake.

They must be given room to operate – act, innovate and test – but they should also be disciplined enough to work within a formal control and reporting system. A framework of 'loose-tight' controls helps to motivate action, stimulate ambition and reward endeavour while retaining control. This careful balance in managing managers is crucial to success.

Part Two

6. Restructuring internal operations

A number of projects may combine to change the business model, revamp outdated processes, to make people and plant more efficient and to do things in the best possible way.

6 Restructuring internal operations

The plan into effect

The aims are fixed, the team is in place, the programme is published, and communication has prepared minds and raised expectations. The next four sections describe the main fields of activity.

In a transformational project, the plan will comprise all four. In a turnaround project, it is likely that major change will either be internal or will focus on customers. Working on both of these simultaneously requires much more effort.

Where a transformational scale is contemplated, the project may need to move more slowly and take longer.

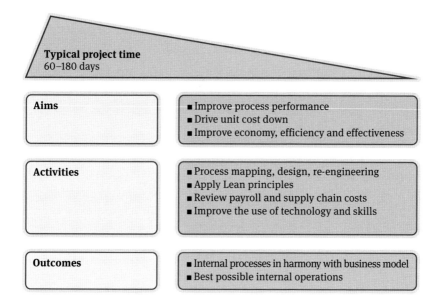

Typical project time
60–180 days

| Aims | ■ Improve process performance
■ Drive unit cost down
■ Improve economy, efficiency and effectiveness |

| Activities | ■ Process mapping, design, re-engineering
■ Apply Lean principles
■ Review payroll and supply chain costs
■ Improve the use of technology and skills |

| Outcomes | ■ Internal processes in harmony with business model
■ Best possible internal operations |

Processes

The baseline investigation will show whether processes need radical change, or whether profits will increase if existing processes are made more efficient.

A new or modified business model may change many aspects of operations. There may be fundamental questions about what markets and customers want, and what has to be done inside the company to satisfy them. The answers to these questions will shape the design of new processes:

- What are the core internal capabilities that give us competitive advantage?
- How do our customers expect us to serve them?
- Which components/products would it be better to procure externally?
- Where should we manufacture and/or assemble?
- What skills are required for manufacturing or providing a service – and do we possess them?
- What are the risks of an extended supply chain?
- Would a partnership or alliance be a sensible approach to designing the supply chain?

There are questions here that need to be answered in terms of structure, capability and location – where should processes be performed, by whom and how?

Lean improvement

The techniques of re-engineering and Lean value-chains are described more fully in our companion volume Managing Productivity. These tools and techniques will help both to create new processes and improve existing ones.

Using a 'Lean' training programme to cut costs

The case study below illustrates some of the elements of the Lean method.

Putting Lean into practice

A company wanted to use training in Lean manufacturing to give managers the skills to investigate every element in the business's value chain. Using these skills, they could then specify and 'charter' projects to improve working practices and to reduce costs. The business wanted to find cost savings of 5 per cent per year and to cut inventory.

The management team followed a structured programme in which they:

- *defined the project, set priorities and determined the resources needed*
- *reviewed the current situation, assessed performance and mapped processes*
- *decided the ideal future state and developed the projects to achieve this*
- *prioritised the projects and developed charters setting out methods and targets, having recognised what customers needed.*

Lean techniques were used to concentrate on processes where most improvement could be achieved, harnessing the enthusiasm, skills and experience of the workforce. This included assessing customers' needs, mapping the flow of materials and information, reviewing data on performance and costs, measuring lead-time and capacity, and investigating errors. Managers also investigated suppliers, measured their performance, and recognised components and processes that might be outsourced at lower costs or better quality.

Multiple projects were outlined to cut costs, reduce inventory and improve lead-times for orders. They embraced better purchasing, selective outsourcing and improvement in processes and working practices. Total projected savings exceeded the target.

Critical judgements

Walking around an operational unit, what do you see? Is it a hive of activity, people in huddles, raw materials and work in progress in abundance, noticeboards full of graphs and exhortations, machines and processes set to work, lots of technical paperwork, an exciting sense of crises being resolved? Is it possible to know what is going on and how good the results are?

Inefficiency shows up in many easily observed ways:

- Untidiness and poor housekeeping
- People walking about or standing in huddles
- Lack of clarity in the flow of work
- Badly categorised orders and materials
- Lack of quality control
- Badly marked out work flows, gangways and storage areas
- Out-of-date graphs, announcements and reports on noticeboards
- Poor timekeeping and attendance
- Dirty washrooms and toilets

Lean programmes measure and change processes by seeing the trends in total unit costs and the profitability of products throughout the organisation, and not department by department in isolation.

Applying Lean principles to operations can, for example, help managers:

- to make effective use of space and equipment. Unused areas are always marked off to create pressure for them to be used more efficiently
- to organise speedy changeovers to cut downtime
- to separate products in large batches from those with short or infrequent runs
- to allocate materials, components and part-finished products in fixed amounts to marked areas
- to prepare simple documents that anyone with limited experience can follow
- to show clearly the productivity of processes and labour and the material yields.

Process mapping

A mapping exercise is the best method of developing an understanding of what actually takes place in the office or on the shop floor. It goes beyond what can be fully understood by managers doing their day-to-day work in that location. There is more to be learned from a mapping exercise than by any other method of investigating activity in the workplace.

The snag is that it takes time and therefore can be expensive. The opportunity for restructuring may have ceased long before this type of detailed analysis is complete. Furthermore, many managers see process mapping as a dull task, beneath their dignity. When done well, documentation can be painstaking in its detail.

❝The temptation to form premature theories upon insufficient data is the bane of our profession.❞
Sherlock Holmes

For restructuring, where rapid change is usually sought, the answer is to be selective about subjects. The benefits to the project have to be worth the time and effort. The principal criterion, as always, is cost. The investigation should have its focus where processes are most costly or critical.

Process investigations are best done by teams made up of those who do the work and know it best, and analysts with a mastery of mapping techniques. It helps if the people who work with the processes can become enthusiastic about the outcome and fully appreciate the chance to improve.

A more rapid but rough and ready technique, known as 'brown-papering', can indicate if more detailed mapping is justified. To do this all the documents and reports relevant to a process are attached to a length of brown paper. Arrows and lines are drawn to show the links and relationships between documents and the data they contain. This can be displayed with dramatic impact. Complexity, repetition, errors and rework can be seen clearly.

The important relationship between service/product and cost of process, known as cost drivers, is illustrated below.

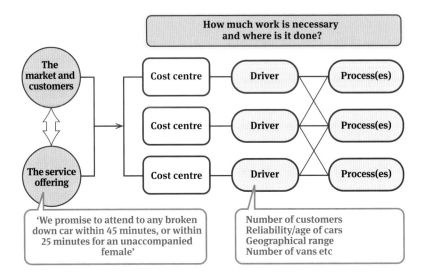

This analysis allows managers to build up a cost model from first principles – driving out cost by 'zero-based budgeting' without losing sight of what is being delivered to the customer.

An accurate evaluation has to be made of what work needs to be done in a defined period: how this is broken down into different tasks; how long each task should take; what allowances should be built in for supervision, management, training, absence etc; what support functions are necessary (HR, finance, purchasing) and what their cost will be. A useful starting point is a map outlining how customers are served, what separate cost centres are involved, what the main drivers of costs are, and the key processes.

This should provide a robust model to find out the best size and shape of the process or business unit, and hence its cost. But it relies heavily on managers describing precisely what work needs to be done and how much effort is necessary to do it. Judgements need to be made strictly on robust evidence and objective reasoning.

The model of costs can be compared with the actual costs, and hypotheses developed about how savings can be made. Potentially the review can take in a wide canvas of core processes, procured materials, overheads, technology and employment practices.

The simple steps towards building a plan for savings are illustrated below.

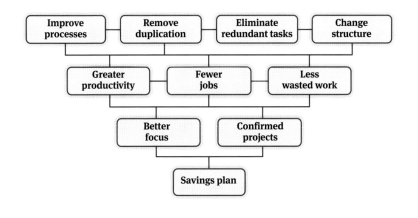

Payroll cost

Payroll structure

A restructuring project is a good opportunity to change the relationship between the cost of people and the company's total cost. In service industries, people represent the biggest single cost. Restructuring may start a new trend towards reducing that cost.

The aims of restructuring should include making payroll more flexible so that it falls or grows in relation to the amount of work to be done. It should look at ways of limiting the total costs of employing people while paying well to attract the type of skills needed. Overall earnings need to bear a sensible relationship to output.

Nearly all pay structures distort over time, and often no longer serve the true aims of the business. Managers make tactical, one-off exceptions to the rules and shape of the structure, ignoring it when it serves their purpose. Most tinkering results in higher rather than lower pay, so the result is a serious drain on profit. Restructuring provides a rationale for review and the chance to link pay to performance.

Better measures and controls throughout the business will determine where it is possible and sensible to create performance-related rewards and how they should work. Careful maintenance of reward structures is essential – they can rapidly become ineffectual when circumstances change.

Differentials in pay may be troublesome for both employees and managers. Modern grading systems often contain too many grade steps, which encourages employees to fabricate responsibilities in which managers are often complicit. Simple structures give the most scope for flexible working – the ability to move employees around within the company without argument, and in and out of employment easily as business ebbs and flows.

Terms and conditions of employment

The baseline investigation should have revealed any obvious inconsistencies and scope for rationalising. Sometimes the case for restructuring will itself suggest a more cost-effective solution to the pay structure by improving the link between reward and work.

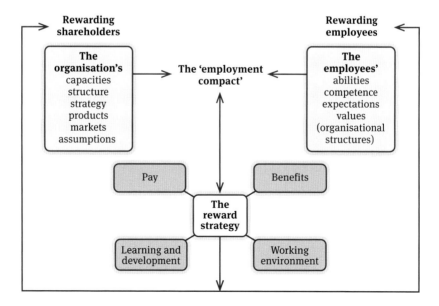

It is not only the number of employees that determines the payroll element of process costs. Rates of pay, including overtime, benefits and the amount of time they spend effectively also count. Obstacles to cutting payroll costs include:

- Pay drift – poor controls on pay inevitably lead to higher than planned costs. 'One-off' benefits are always worthy of further examination.
- Recruitment and selection – in many companies, poorly coordinated recruitment processes lead to duplication and higher costs. In tight labour markets managers seriously underestimate the cost of finding recruits.
- Unproductive time – the analysis will reveal the proportion of time being spent on meetings, travel, managing e-mail, social events and other activities of questionable benefit. The underlying rationale must be challenged.
- Use of temporary and contract workers – many firms that use agency workers do not know what they cost and do not manage their performance. Are contract employees' costs counted as payroll or purchases?
- Overtime (paid or unpaid) – too much or too little use of overtime indicates poor apportioning between people and tasks. There should always be slightly more work than people to do it.
- Managerial time – a comparison of how managers in different parts of the firm use their time can be revealing. Signs that they spend a significant amount of time on the same tasks as subordinates should be challenged.

Changes to the 'employment package' will require negotiation and take time. But restructuring provides the opportunity for multiple changes. New circumstances, like changes to hours, the content of jobs and location, may need a review of terms and conditions.

Outsourcing

No restructuring project should fail to investigate the possible benefits of reshaping processes, organisational structure and resources by buying goods or services instead of creating them.

Not even core processes have to be performed within the business itself. This is not confined to activities such as finance and HR, but applies to supply chain and manufacturing also. There is just as much opportunity in service industries.

For example, insurance companies outsource multiple specific skills. Marketing is outsourced to agents like banks and the post office as well as to retail brokers; claims are outsourced to claims handlers and assessors; risk assessment is outsourced to medical screeners and credit agencies; and risks are underwritten by Lloyds and others. As another example, oil companies outsource exploration, drilling and other operations.

> **❝**Complex processes are by their very definition rigid, inflexible, low quality, and high cost.**❞**
> **Michael Hammer**

The benefits of outsourcing need to be secured by rigorously selecting contractors and retaining full control over their costs and effectiveness. The decision whether to outsource part or all of a process poses some fundamental questions:

- How important is possessing operational expertise to the future of our business?
- Is it feasible to outsource the supply of components or ingredients of our product?
- Can we retain enough expertise to manage a new supplier so that quality is not compromised?
- What impact will this have on our position in the market?
- Will we be able to serve our customers in the same way – and will they notice or care?
- High-value supplies can be sent by air, but many others need to go by road or sea. What impact will this have on our responsiveness in the market and our ability to modify or customise products and hold inventory?
- Will this result in the price paid by our customers falling? What effects will that have on our relative and absolute margins?
- What will be the true annual savings per year, taking into account potential reductions in sales prices, increases in supply chain costs, increases in working capital and loss of responsiveness?
- Is our proprietary technology, intellectual property or expertise at risk?

Procurement

The aggressive buyer, driven by price (at all costs!), is a common source of fear and respect. However, the best price very often does not lead to the lowest overall cost.

By way of example, an ambitious buyer of aluminium was keen to drive down the purchase price per unit by accepting delivery of a year's supply. The business had the warehouse space to do this. But nobody had told the buyer that the specification was about to change or that this particular aluminium had a limited shelf life. In this case the consequences were dire, but mistakes of this type are not uncommon.

Problems are caused in part by withholding communications about strategy and plans from buyers who are thought to be too junior to be trusted. Some purchasing professionals are unwilling to get out of their offices to learn how the things they buy are used, sold and bought by customers.

The restructuring programme should look closely at the decision-making process for purchasing, as this is where savings usually lie, waiting for a systematic investigation.

Checklist for reducing costs

Materials
- Improved procurement practices
- Better materials utilisation
- Cheaper substitute materials
- Functional design changes to components
- Change to product design principles

Payroll
- Changes in the line reporting structure (layers and spans and managers)
- Forced headcount reduction of both direct and indirect processes
  - natural wastage
  - recruitment freeze
  - early retirement
  - voluntary redundancy
  - reduced overtime working

- ➤ revised shift patterns
- ➤ short-time working
- ➤ work sharing
- ➤ transfers to other duties
- ➤ outsource to cheaper unit
- ■ Reduce pay
  - ➤ wage cut deals
  - ➤ bonus cut deals
  - ➤ pay freeze
  - ➤ reduce or freeze benefits
  - ➤ reform grade structures, assign lower grades of labour to process or change grade mix
- ■ Process improvement by Lean tools and techniques
  - ➤ automation
  - ➤ new technology
  - ➤ work rate
  - ➤ motivational techniques and incentives
  - ➤ training and improved skills
  - ➤ performance incentives
  - ➤ overheads of people – see payroll on previous page and above
- ■ Organisational structure – close, combine, share departments and resources, remove duplication
  - ➤ outsource functions
  - ➤ reduce energy consumption
  - ➤ save on procurement
  - ➤ property – cut budgets for repair and maintenance, outsource facilities management, space utilisation
  - ➤ sites – consolidate, close, mothball, import tenancies, sale and lease-back
  - ➤ R&D – cut budgets, reorder priorities, outsource
  - ➤ IT Systems – cut budgets, reorder priorities
  - ➤ outsource, cease in-house development and use proprietary software

7. Serving customers better

Increasing the competitiveness of the business means serving customers better with the right products or services in the best way.

7 Serving customers better

Competitiveness

Competitiveness is at the heart of every business model. Restructuring will generate tasks ranging from minor modifications in the service to customers, to radical shifts in product offerings or the markets served.

Often most of the changes – to management, costs, organisation, sites and locations, and the workforce – are internal.

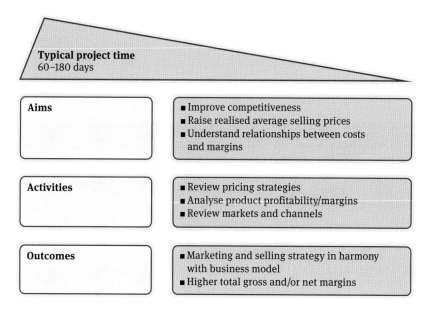

Typical project time
60–180 days

| Aims | ■ Improve competitiveness
■ Raise realised average selling prices
■ Understand relationships between costs and margins |

| Activities | ■ Review pricing strategies
■ Analyse product profitability/margins
■ Review markets and channels |

| Outcomes | ■ Marketing and selling strategy in harmony with business model
■ Higher total gross and/or net margins |

Pricing

Quick wins

With constant volumes, price is the single biggest influence on profit. Small changes to price cause big changes to the bottom line. In a typical manufacturing business, a 1 per cent increase in price can often raise profits by as much as 25 per cent. Despite the leverage that prices give to financial results, most companies spend little time and use scant resources to manage pricing as a commercial task.

Although a marketing strategy may take time to develop and implement, the opportunity to raise prices may not need to wait. Sometimes this is an opportunity recognised most quickly by new leaders, post-acquisition, than by incumbent managers who have a much more long-standing relationship with customers to whom they may, over time, become indulgent. This is often the first business decision of new broom executives after they take charge.

A restructuring project can take this shortcut to financial transformation seriously. Blanket rises in price are not the only option. Selective increases and restructuring the tariff may have the same effect and generate less reaction from customers. Watering down the specification has the same effect, such as smaller chocolate bars sold at the same price.

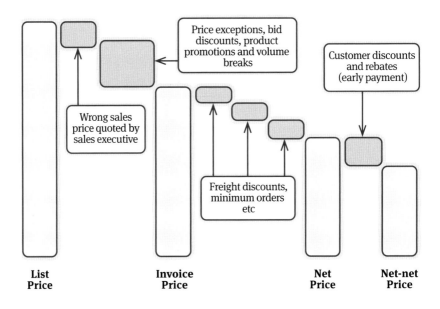

Missed opportunities

Failing to establish or to sustain a pricing policy inevitably weakens performance. The value of relationships with customers is undermined, so competitors in market segments that are more sensitive to price can quickly prosper.

How do these problems occur? In many cases,

the root cause is the fragmentation of the pricing
process throughout the organisation.

Marketing typically establishes list or gross prices, bundles, products and features, and sets the general outline for promotional incentive programmes. Sales then set net prices in a number of ways: by offering specific incentives by distributor, channel or customer; by relaxing contractual agreements; and by creating other discounts designed to match or beat competitors' offers.

Many other factors are often not even considered in the 'pricing equation', but are determined by the Finance and Operations departments, whose decisions, in effect, offer services at a set or discounted price. For example, Finance will stipulate the payment terms and financing options. Operations will set the terms for minimum orders and freight charges. Finally, Customer Service has the difficult responsibility of enforcing (or not enforcing) pricing policies and it must also resolve quality problems and disputes over the prices and quantities on invoices.

By the time all departments have had their say, the effective net price is far from the original list or intended net price. The illustration shows how uncoordinated pricing decisions can reduce margins.

Pricing strategy

As well as providing the opportunity for a quick fix, restructuring also provides a genuine opportunity to organise a more thorough review of pricing. For example, when a product or service has become undifferentiated, most purchasers have a perception of value associated with the price they are prepared to pay. The pricing strategy should explore the notion of value in terms of price and cost, and non-price differentiators such as the speed and quality of service.

Pricing is the centre ground of the whole marketing mix. Every expression of value relates to it. To get to the heart of this we need to research profitability in the ways described below.

Profitability

Margins

Profitability is usually measured at gross margin – revenue or selling price after charging the variable cost of production or supply. Net margin can also be calculated after selling or channel costs have been allocated, if a meaningful attribution can be made.

The key to profit planning is capturing this knowledge by product, customer and market attributes.

Products and product groups by:
- customers
- channels to market
- market sectors and sub-sectors, and
- origin of manufacture or supply.

Customers and customer types by:
- geographical distribution
- size
- purchased value and volume, and
- market sector.

Markets by:
- size
- sector
- number of players
- end users, and
- channels served.

> *"I'm the only person I know that's lost a quarter of a billion dollars in one year... It's very character-building."*
>
> **Steve Jobs**

If the company's information systems can provide data of this richness it will have the means to develop product and market strategies with precision. Acquiring, installing and populating a new information system with good data may in some cases take up to a year. If there is no revenue or profit crisis, this time may be available and the effort worthwhile. Outcomes from restructuring information and systems can take more time than any other change to processes.

Data and tools

Modelling tools that capture and process data by attribute, as described above, can show which products, and in which markets, margins can offer the best percentage return and, when multiplied by sales volume, which of them are creating the most total value for the business.

But in a complete model to support sales and marketing strategy, other factors have to be introduced such as variations in price, volume, competitor reaction, market share and so on. Modern systems will source these data from the sales ledger. To calculate a true margin, the database will also need to be populated with standard product costs.

In the absence of database tools, it is still possible to construct a less sophisticated model from data cut and assembled with 'knife and fork'. But this slow, hard work is difficult to justify given the potential return from investing in software that will give better results faster.

Analysis

To restructure and rebuild a platform for profitability, a business needs to be able to model the effects of changes to cost, price, mix and volume on margins. This sometimes provides an authoritative basis for challenging managers' instincts and prejudices where there are difficult decisions to cull products. Many companies carry products and services in the range that are not justified by the margins earned on them or the volume sold. Often analysis reveals the cause of low margins to be costs that have not previously been recognised or understood. For example, analysis can uncover:

- products and services that are failing to make sufficient contribution to overhead and profit after selling and channel costs
- the need to raise prices as a tactic to speed up product withdrawal from a range
- the chance to increase selling prices, particularly of products with strategic importance to customers
- special or low-volume products and services with underestimated costs not reflected in the price
- second-string products and services with lower volume and high unit costs that possibly should be subcontracted in order to set and hold a higher margin.

When products are discontinued, there should be a search for the fixed costs that support them, which should then be cut.

Marketing strategy

What does a marketing strategy look like in a post-acquisition restructuring? The following powerful example is taken from a real case.

Challenging the profitability of 'popular' brands

The acquirer of a tobacco company with a large market share and many popular brands but low return on sales and capital, studied the market and developed a radical strategy.

First, the number of product lines was severely reduced after profitability was analysed. The remaining products were then supported by heavy advertising.

Secondly, market share, regarded by the previous leadership as its measure of success, was abandoned as a measure of performance, and share permitted to fall substantially. Profitability per line became the measure of accountability.

Thirdly, manufacturing was restructured around the smaller number of product lines, and unit costs driven down. Manufacturing sites were closed. There was heavy investment in the best available technology.

Freed from the shackles of an excessive range and high unit costs of production, total profit peaked despite historically low sales revenue.

After five years, reinvested profit was creating unrivalled competitiveness, with the return of high market share and industry-leading margins.

Costing and marketing

Traditional costing

The purpose of product and process costing is not to determine the price to be charged but to understand the profitability of the product at any given price and volume. Systems for costing manufactured products have always been a blind spot in much of UK industry. Many firms consider a product cost to be the labour, materials and recovery of overhead. Process cost rates are built up in much the same way. Overhead has often been charged to product using bizarre formulas, such as a percentage of direct labour, or direct material, or even sales value.

It is often thought that costs that do not vary with volume (indirect costs) should be allocated to products. This is to avoid underpricing them and misjudging the sales required for the recovery of those costs. However, this approach tends to focus effort on increasing sales volume rather than on the need to hold down the 'fixed' overhead cost itself. It feeds the dangerous concept of marginal costing and pricing, and invites inappropriate ways of allocating or attributing any overhead cost which is unrelated to the production, procurement or provision of product or service.

This method may give some idea of average costs at an assumed volume. But it will always fail to attribute enough cost to low-volume, complex products, and often attributes too much to high-volume, less complex ones. The latter can then become overpriced and uncompetitive, and sales volume falls. Orders for underpriced low-volume specials may rise, as will losses. Often it is better not to allocate overheads at all, but to set a higher target percentage margin, and to budget volume at a level sufficient to yield enough net margin (or contribution to overheads and profit) to give the net profit and financial return that is wanted.

Activity-based costing

Activity-based costing sets out to tackle the problem in a different way. It removes the concept of fixed and indirect costs and, in practice, assumes all costs to be variable. Then all the costs and overheads of the resources associated with each activity can be apportioned using the precise tools that activity-based costing employs. In this way it becomes possible to evaluate the benefits and costs of changes to products and processes on a fully absorbed basis.

Though attractive in concept, activity-based costing can be difficult to put in place. It needs a great deal of detailed investigation. Too many data and a large product range can keep an army of analysts busy, and create a complex costing model that needs continual maintenance. If too few data are put into the model the result will be no better than a conventional costing system. Rather than running activity-based costing every month, it can be better value to use it in periodic investigations to reset baseline costs.

Where cost information has never been available, or has been absent for a long time and is now critical for analysing the profitability of product and process, activity-based costing may fit in with a restructuring programme.

Equivalent units

Another approach to searching for the costs of products is to establish the relative conversion costs of all the products made in a single factory. This makes it possible to show the impact on product cost of planned changes in the mix of products. This also gives managers a way of measuring absolute changes in productivity over a lengthy period, such as several years. It has been known to encourage a fundamental change in the attitude of managers and shop-floor employees to improving long-term productivity.

The equivalent units technique is to take the total unit conversion costs (excluding material) of each product. Then the total unit conversion cost of the product with the highest annual volume is set at one 'equivalent unit', and all other products are given relative 'equivalent unit' values to it.

At the outset, the total annual costs of all the output will equate to the total conversion costs included in the equivalent units. From this point these equivalent unit costs are used to measure the total value of output.

The method can also be used to create budgets and to assist investment strategy directed at products.

8. Accountability and performance

Improving the accountability of managers has a profound effect on the outcomes of restructuring projects.

8 Accountability and performance

For every process an accountable manager

A programme of restructuring must consider the strength of the regime for holding managers to account. The first question to be asked is what managers are to be held accountable for, and then by what means, and how performance against accountability should be measured.

The accountability of managers must relate directly to the processes for which they have responsibility. But in practice there is often a failure to match all processes with all managers: there are always some processes, or parts of them, for which no manager has responsibility, and thus there will be no accountability for its performance.

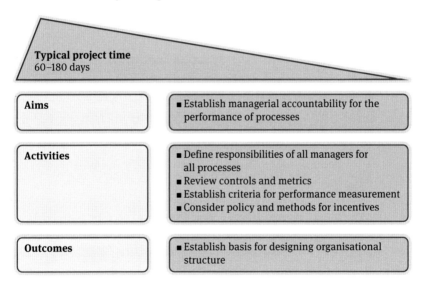

Typical project time
60–180 days

Aims	■ Establish managerial accountability for the performance of processes
Activities	■ Define responsibilities of all managers for all processes ■ Review controls and metrics ■ Establish criteria for performance measurement ■ Consider policy and methods for incentives
Outcomes	■ Establish basis for designing organisational structure

Reporting performance

Careful design of internal business reports – management information, profit and loss accounts and balance sheets – helps to avoid holes and mismatches. Where they are found, either the system and mechanics of reporting, or the design and properties of the measures, or both, will need to be amended as a vital aspect of the restructuring programme.

If a restructuring project changes the processes of a business then the accountabilities of managers and the measures of performance for which they are held accountable will also require overhaul. The type and degree of change required in reporting performance may depend on how much the organisational structure has evolved in either or both its managerial and business unit forms. This is described later.

❝Beware lest you lose the substance by grasping at the shadow.❞

Aesop

Controls

Controls are the reports used to communicate performance to managers. They allow results to be interpreted and action encouraged.

The quality and design of performance reporting about managers, processes and units of the business rests on the organisation's management accounting capability. If this expertise is not up to scratch then reporting on business performance will be bland and uninformative before restructuring takes place, and will not improve afterwards unless the restructuring programme adds a project accounting capability. Improving the way in which the business is reported should nearly always be near the top of the list of restructuring reforms.

The aim should be to have the monthly profit and loss account built up from a series of subsidiary reports, each of which speaks to, and cross references the performance of, the senior managerial accountabilities. The subsidiary reports should reach down far enough to ensure that all managers and their accountabilities are covered.

Reports should 'nest' in the same way as the managerial structure is configured, so that profit and loss is transparently the sum of all the reportable units for which managers are accountable. It is an important part of any restructuring programme to put this firmly in place where it has previously been slack.

Metrics

This is not the place for a complete survey of metrics, but how they are used in programmes of restructuring is important. A project should investigate the following:

■ How relevant are the metrics to the overall performance of the business?
■ Do they measure the degree to which managers control the activity and processes for which they have accountability?
■ Are there enough metrics, or even too many?
■ Are there reliable data on performance? Are they consistent, appropriate, economic to collect and auditable?

Examples of metrics include: return on capital employed, average selling price, and payroll cost per employee hour worked. Measures can, and ought to be designed as a hierarchy so that the ones at operational level tie in with those that monitor policy and financial performance. This implies a nesting or dovetailing of metrics all the way up the managerial hierarchy.

The diagram suggests how metrics need to be designed:

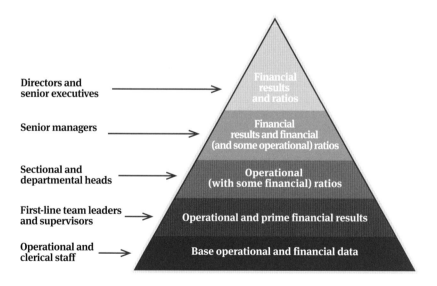

Balanced scorecards

The challenge to reporting a number of performance indices is to assess whether an improvement in one is comparable or even compatible with that in another. At a high degree of sophistication, it may be practical to build an econometric model that combines the results mathematically, following the structure of the management accounts. But the creation of such a formula may demand too many good data, and too much testing to justify the effort.

Balanced scorecards can achieve the equivalent effect. The indices in each chosen set are given a (usually estimated) weighting to reflect their relative importance. A set of, say, ten indices can be combined into a single score that indicates a clear trend. Movements in the trend can be investigated by studying the changes in the various indices. The table below suggests the idea.

Objectives	Indices	Units	Performance			Score
			Current	Target	Weighting	
Financials	a Sales b Gross margin c Cash					
Customers	a Satisfaction b Churn c Acquisition rate					
Internal processes	a Error rates b Productivity ratios c Cost reduction rate					
Learning and growth	a Capability framework b Qualifications c Development projects					
					Total	

Trend, and the tracking of it, is usually more important to the business as a whole than the absolute measure of achievement for any single period by an individual manager.

The impact of restructuring can be assessed through the prism of the changes in scorecard metrics. The business case for restructuring should have set a baseline.

Performance bridges

To report changes over a period, including at each stage of a restructuring project and from its start to its finish, performance bridges illustrate movements from the baseline to end point. For example:

- by the contribution from different business units, sector markets, geographies, sites/plants, lines of business, et cetera
- by root cause – price, volume, gross margin, overhead cost reduction, et cetera
- by each initiative within the project overall.

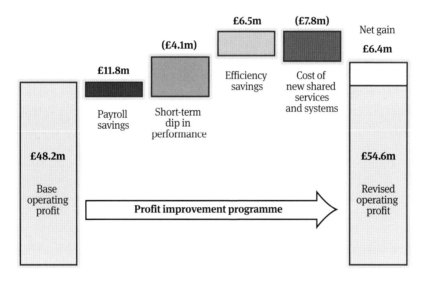

The performance bridge is a powerful means of holding any manager or group of managers to account including, for example, a restructuring team or project group accountable for measurable results with multiple factors of influence. Used in conjunction with a project 'scorecard', it should be aligned with the management accounts to explain the effect of other variances and/or reflect changes of tactics.

Comparison of the performance bridge projected at the outset of a restructuring exercise with the final picture will show to what extent the initial plans have been translated into firm, measurable results.

Giving managers an incentive

A restructuring project is fertile ground for incentivising managers. The anticipated improvement in financial performance offers ample potential benefits that can be attached to highly geared rewards based on outcomes.

Incentives influence behaviours. Or at least they do if they have a specific purpose and are properly designed. Problems with incentives arise less from the principle but from decisions about what behaviour they are intended to promote. Incentives are at their most effective when given to those with responsibility for leadership.

For example there is no need to incentivise a whole department if the same effect can be obtained, at less cost, by incentivising its leader. If a supervisor controls how smoothly a process works and that is the key constraint on output, then that is where the incentive should be aimed.

Schemes for payment by results come in generic types which need some differentiation. For example, there are personal incentives whose design is to stretch mangers to be high-performing achievers. And there are sharing schemes more democratically designed to encourage a climate of active engagement among employees (as at John Lewis). Both work. But each is designed to achieve something different.

Payments by results need to be self-financing – they need to cost a good deal less than the benefit accrued by the business. They should be closely related to the measures of business performance that matter most and directly affect profit.

The size of bonus and shape of any sliding scale, the starting point for payment, limits (if any), and qualifying conditions are all technical decisions that need a professional understanding of the subject to ensure mistakes are not made. In no field of management can harmony turn so quickly to dissatisfaction as in the design of a bonus scheme that begins or appears to go off the rails, leaving one or both parties feeling cheated.

Targets should be reviewed from year to year so that they remain consonant with the needs and aspirations of the business.

9. Designing organisational structure

It is best to understand fully the business model and how its core processes work before committing to a new structure.

9   Designing organisational structure

Build structures with caution

It may seem strange to have left organisational design as the last of the four main fields of restructuring activity. Many companies undergoing restructuring start with a new structure and then design everything else around it. Even the terms organisational structure and restructuring are often used synonymously.

The truth is that change to how the organisation is put together should recognise the modular nature of processes and the way they flow and fit together. Put another way, the natural and best available design of process flow should determine the way managerial jobs are organised. Executives whose jobs are detached from processes cannot be mainstream managers. The design of processes defines the jobs by which they are managed. A good example of this is presented by processes that flow across more than one site. The popular approach is to focus on the site as the basis for appointing managers at that level. But a structure that follows the geography in that way may be less successful than another rooted in accountability for processes operating across more than one site. Having one responsible manager per site is almost certainly wrong in these circumstances because it will emphasise location rather than process excellence.

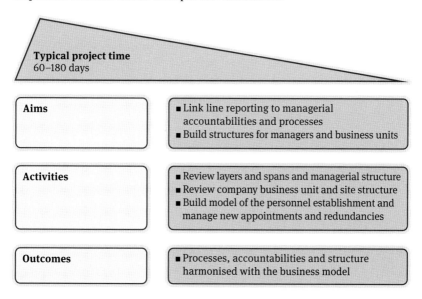

Typical project time
60–180 days

Aims	■ Link line reporting to managerial accountabilities and processes ■ Build structures for managers and business units
Activities	■ Review layers and spans and managerial structure ■ Review company business unit and site structure ■ Build model of the personnel establishment and manage new appointments and redundancies
Outcomes	■ Processes, accountabilities and structure harmonised with the business model

In the same way, measuring profit by site will say less than measuring it (or the cost) by process. Sites themselves are not necessarily a logical stream of revenue or profit. They do not necessarily make or lose money per se and may be better judged as economic or uneconomic depending on whether they succeed or fail in optimising unit costs.

Thus it is wrong to assume that sites are profit centres and site managers are profit centre managers. If it is not possible to report the performance of processes, assets or managers meaningfully then the organisational structure is likely to be incorrect and the wrong results measured.

Line reporting and accountability

The position of important executives in the structure needs to be planned and put in place as soon as possible so that managers can get on with change. Managers need:

- clear accountabilities and design of jobs
- appropriate pay and incentives, if appropriate
- appropriate contracts.

There should be no room for doubt about how the restructured business is to be managed and where responsibility for operational and financial control and profit will reside. How lines of reporting lie should indicate how the business is meant to work.

Surprisingly charts often fail to indicate how processes and people are actually managed. People say that charts lie: 'it shows I report to him but that is not how it is'; and A says B reports to him, but B says C is his manager.

To restructure the organisation, the chart must show how jobs fit with processes, and how accountability is exercised, reported and measured. If A is not accountable for the performance of the process and B manages the process, then B cannot and ought not to report to A, whatever A says.

This sounds like common sense. But the logic of managerial structures is not put to this test in many companies. Examples of this are found in all organisations where no management audit has been attempted. If restructuring does approach organisational configuration in this way there is often an added bonus: behavioural problems, which so often drag down the performance of managers, will diminish.

Accountability

What managers do must be consistent with the results they want. The 'right structure' is crucial. General Schwarzkopf insisted that one person (General Pagonis) be in charge of all logistics. This contrasted with the divided accountabilities of all previous campaigns. Said Pagonis, 'decentralisation without somebody being held responsible does not work'. The need, in his words, is 'centralised control with decentralised execution'.

Collinson Grant calls this 'loose/tight' managing. The organisational structure must not get in the way of process and accountability.

Decisions about a new structure should be communicated as early as possible. They will help to clarify which skills are needed in the new business, which jobs will remain, which new ones will be created and which ones are likely to go.

At the same time, it is useful to set out any implications for changes in terms and conditions of employment (subject to local legislation) and the impact on pay and prospects. This can help to reduce stress, which may be damaging to productivity, and will help to retain staff that are important to the new structure.

Layers and spans

The 'shape' of an organisation does much to determine its effectiveness and cost. Wide, flat structures tend to be more efficient than tall, narrow ones. Many firms have too many people with managerial status (and pay) who have no clearly defined managerial accountability. This results in higher costs, inflexible responses and lower productivity.

Fewer managerial layers make for flatter and more cost-effective structures that speed communication from the top to the bottom and from the bottom up, and improve it qualitatively. Flatter structures promote a better focus on accountability, reducing the need for multiple degrees of delegation. More layers devolve responsibility for measurable outputs.

It is the job of managers to be responsible for the work of others. If they do the same tasks as those they manage, they are more likely to be 'team leaders.' Those who do specialised work or are classed as 'expert' and manage or supervise very few others, or none at all, should not be regarded as managers, and should be repositioned in the structure so they do not complicate the structure and interfere with the upwards and downwards passage of communication.

Focusing organisational structure on the market

A large manufacturer of mobile plant for rough terrain had four manufacturing divisions – transmissions, lower power train, hydraulics and steering, and controls. Each activity took place in its own factory, although many generic processes were found at more than one of the locations. There was a general manager for each division. Each division included procurement, engineering design, system integrators and sales engineers. A search for a better relationship between cost and added value concluded that the divisional structure could be changed and cost saved by reducing duplication in the factories and divisions. The new structure put all manufacturing under a single general manager, allowing factories and production processes to be rationalised with improvement to economy and efficiency.

Procurement, engineering design and engineering support to sales were then organised along product and market lines with three market-facing general managers. This improved the effectiveness of the value chain of each product by strengthening relationships with customers and improving the design of products, as the engineering needs of different markets became better understood. This had to be accompanied by changes in the design of managers' jobs, measurement and accountabilities as well as in the business and managerial structures.

Business units

Value chain

The principal influence on how business units in a company, or group, are configured is the value chain. This is where companies create wealth through a sequence of linked processes. But processes can be often be joined up end to end in different ways, from the purchased inputs at one end of the chain to delivered product or service at the other. Every company should be able to recognise its own value chain configuration. This can be the essence of the business model and is a valid expression of its strategies.

The organisation therefore needs to position units of activity around processes in order to give form to its structure. Optimal structures will be those that liberate rather than limit their economy (input of cost), efficiency (output for the given input) and effectiveness (overall qualitative and quantitative output). But what does that mean?

For example, a company manufacturing on three sites could organise itself so that each site is a separate cost centre. This would configure the accountability of managers geographically by putting under their control all those processes and resources needed to produce their end product.

Alternatively, the configuration could be designed to reflect functionality by, for example, placing accountability for machining on all of the three sites under a single point of managerial control, with units for assembly, testing and packaging treated similarly. This may shorten the part of the value chain over which any plant-based production manager has control. Such a decision implies creating a business unit with, for example, the accountability for managing product from material and parts purchase, design, and channel to market.

Similar decisions would be needed in considering a structure for sales, where choices exist for organising accountability and measurement by geography, or customers by type, or channels to market. Restructuring offers the opportunity to study options for configuration that might modify the strategy to get the best business performance.

Profit centres

How and where profit is to be managed and measured is a critical factor in organisational design. In concept the profit centre is a self-contained, relatively autonomous unit whose leader (chief executive, managing director, unit manager or even depot manager) has accountabilities linked to a budgeted profit. The profit centre manager needs to have enough power to make independent decisions on those factors that determine the profit if the organisational structure is to be meaningful.

For example, there must be a budget for sales, with some influence on prices, product mix and the control of direct costs, so that the profit centre manager is responsible for margins and most of the overheads so that a measurable profit is realised locally. Profit centres can be large – effectively encompassing all the operations of a single medium-sized business of several thousand people or many millions of sales turnover. The principal factor determining whether to subdivide a company into profit centre building blocks is whether accountability for a well-defined profit number is possible without stopping its processes from working in the best way.

"*He that will not apply new remedies must expect new evils; for time is the greatest innovator.*"
Francis Bacon

Devolved structures

Devolved structures often duplicate activities and therefore cost. Activity that takes place on a small scale can be less efficient and of less consistent quality. This is not an argument for centralisation. Restructuring in order to give devolved units access to larger, centralised functions with reduced unit costs can be made possible by, for example, creating shared services units or by outsourcing them.

Devolved units can encourage greater entrepreneurial behaviour and bind organisations into closer relationships with customers. Equally they can reduce the power of brands and reputation, lead to the uncoordinated implementation of strategy, permit independence to degrade into ill-discipline, or suffer outbreaks of territorialism.

Operator and trader structure

Some of the biggest impacts from restructuring can result from adopting an organisational structure in which an organisation is designed around the two core functions that every company has:

- its capacity to produce, and
- its need to sell.

The concept is not universally suitable but can flourish at companies and in industries where the imperative of production is to suppress internally generated cost and that of sales is to maximise total margin.

The operational flaw often found in conventionally integrated companies is that sales volume is allowed to become the main driver of production efficiency. The result can be that the volume of production needed to achieve a certain degree of efficiency and unit cost is allowed to determine the minimum acceptable volume of budgeted sales. In a competitive market that can drive down prices and margins – a classic example of the tail (production) wagging the dog (sales).

Symptoms of this are:

- sales budgets are customarily set or validated by production managers
- when unit costs of production rise above the budget number, production managers blame sales staff for not selling enough volume
- when unit costs fall, both sales and production managers claim credit for the same achievement
- accountability for a range of costs seems diffuse – not all money spent has a responsible manager by the time it appears in the profit and loss account
- too many people have the power of discretion over the prices actually paid by customers (no firm price controls)
- actual and budgeted margin percentages are a consequence of decisions on prices and the outcome of costs instead of the other way round

- everyone claims credit for good margins and blames others when they are poor.

The structural solution (also called internal transfer pricing or ITP) is to divide the core of the organisation into two divisions in which:

- one of them, the Operations Division, is accountable for cost effectiveness measured against standardised unit costs that are not affected by the actual level of volume, and
- the other, Trading or Commercial Division, is accountable for achieving targeted total margin at any level of volume.

Operator/trader structure

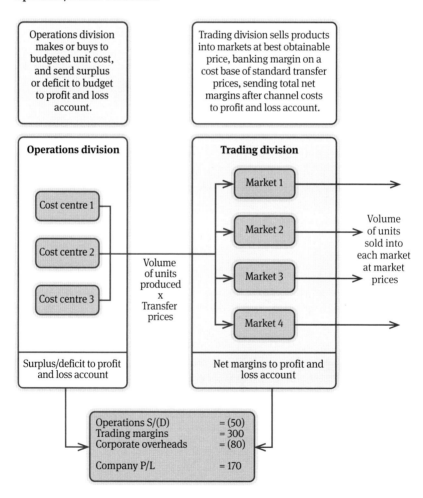

An important aspect of adopting the Operations and Trading structure is the access it gives to robust reporting of managerial performance. Variance analysis is used to understand what has forced any particular business result, and what corrective actions might be needed to get back on track. Reports produce an analysis of variances by volume, cost, mix and price for both Operations and Trading Divisions.

The profit and loss result becomes transparent because it can be seen as the outcome of the performance of different parts of the business, each of which has its clearly defined role.

At the heart of this arrangement is an organisational structure that emphasises clear accountabilities for the different processes. Managerial ownership of costs and margins is unambiguous. Restructuring to this organisational design can put new corporate energy and managerial commitment into a company.

Matrix structures

Hopefully, it will be more common to find restructuring removing a matrix structure than installing it. The potential weakness of this hybrid form of structure is the matrix's defining characteristic, that one manager has equally weighted lines of reporting to two (or possibly more) bosses. It is sometimes alleged that this results in the subordinate manager not being fully accountable to either. But at the least there is an unhealthy weakness in the line reporting.

It is true that this looser structural form is often employed to deal with complex relationships. Other advantages might include the fostering of managerial creativity, providing an environment for teamwork to thrive, and encouraging mature behaviours and decision-making based on consensus. This, it is sometimes said, enables whole managerial groups to act as one, and so adapt quickly to changing conditions in the marketplace and in technology. People with specialist skills can feel particularly comfortable in this type of structure.

History and culture, or the governing dynamic of a business which is often present in its industry, may influence whether the matrix works or not. Organisations focused on fast-moving new technologies may thrive on structures that do not strongly prescribe particular behavioural norms.

However, a matrix structure is rarely a good solution if it is considered culturally important that performances are strictly measured against clear managerial accountabilities. In more mature or conventional businesses a matrix can blur objectivity, hinder effective decision-making, reinforce bureaucracy and undermine accountability.

It is these problems that, over time, can be the cause of a managerial malaise leading to underperformance and the need for the revitalising effects of a restructuring.

> **"***Everything is vague to a degree you do not realise till you have tried to make it precise.***"**
> **Bertrand Russell**

Justifying structural change

To some degree, every change in organisational structure is an experiment. Outcomes are inherently uncertain because finding and implementing the 'best' structure is not the only factor which decides success. The quality of implementation, and the post-implementation behaviours of managers, are both vital influences.

In planning restructuring, it is necessary to consider where advantage best lies. No change of structure is likely to succeed if it makes selling more difficult or reduces sales volume, prices and margins. The impact of structure on those is not necessarily insignificant. The organisational deployment of sales resources and opening up new or improved channels to market can be changed for the better. But it is also easy to reduce the effectiveness of the sales effort by making changes to how it is managed.

Putting a new structure in place

The project plan will determine when the structural changes that affect managers' jobs will take place. Earlier, we suggested that the future for processes and accountabilities should be clear before structure is set in stone.

New organisational charts are not enough to describe the implications associated with a new structure. Managers need to:

- introduce revised managerial accountabilities and staffing
- draw up flow-charts to show the key business processes and sub-processes over which they have been given control
- know the impact of changes in the structure and business processes on relationships with customers and/or suppliers and others
- recognise the main effect of the changes on employees, including any necessary changes to terms and conditions of employment and reward
- assess the principal risks in the proposed change and the actions necessary to mitigate them
- summarise the expected benefits and when they should be realised.

Closure and relocation

Restructuring provides the opportunity to reconsider the justification for the number and location of sites or establishments from which the business operates. Indeed, the project may have been launched with change of this sort in mind. Most companies operating from more than one site will have originally had many good reasons for their locations. These now may have little to do with optimising current cost effectiveness and everything to do with legacy. All other things being equal, a site closure usually saves costs.

Even a closure that is necessary and worthwhile can, however, pose a threat to the business. And yet, during a well-managed closure, performance may actually increase. To that end:

- justify the case for closure – profitable sites are difficult to close
- manage communications and consultation carefully
- administer the procedures scrupulously – in both the spirit and the letter
- maintain good relationships with local officials (and, in certain countries, politicians and journalists)
- form relationships with local businesses that may be able to absorb some of the employees
- help people to find new jobs or retraining
- offer a relatively generous deal and give incentives to employees who stay to the closure date, and achieve the required output, quality and service.

> *"Only the wisest and the stupidest of men never change."*
> **Confucius**

A closure should be managed as an opportunity to establish new ways of working at the host site and to leave behind a sense that the company did everything it could to mitigate circumstances beyond its control.

People adapt quickly to relocation, but retain the memory of how well or badly colleagues were treated.

New locations are chosen for one of three reasons: they may be best for serving the customer by, for example, geographic proximity; they may be well placed to attract executives and employees with special skills; or they may be cheaper to operate.

Managing excess European capacity

A leading manufacturer of paper products reviewed its capacity in Western Europe and decided to consolidate production on fewer sites. So the decision was made to close a long-established mill in southern France.

Consultants helped to bring about closure without disrupting production, at minimum cost, and fully in compliance with complex French employment law. Capacity was maintained by increasing production at a Belgian factory. An interim general manager from Collinson Grant, a French national, ran the factory for ten months and maintained its output. He led sensitive negotiations with the unions, local political leaders and government officers. A Social Plan, which reduced the company's legal and financial exposure, was drafted and accepted. Considerable local opposition to the closure manifested itself in scurrilous publicity, lock-ins and more intimidating measures. But the factory was closed two months ahead of schedule.

The company's managers in the UK had underestimated the complexity of French legal requirements in restructuring, and the potential costs associated with such a project. They were relieved when the plan was

---

realised without serious hindrance to the parent's policy of rationalising the number of locations from which it operated. In the event, the local officials were grateful for the fair and meticulous way in which the closure had been handled and all the adverse aspects of publicity were fully mitigated.

Redundancies

Changing the structure of the organisation often means fewer jobs. This may be a consequence of 'down-sizing' in response to falling demand, or 'right-sizing' to reflect greater efficiency and effectiveness.

Making jobs redundant and parting company with people takes care and attention to detail. Getting it wrong wastes time, distracts managers and can end up being very costly – especially if aggravating circumstances related to discrimination are linked to claims for unfair dismissal.

Managing redundancies well in the circumstances benefits everyone. It fulfils commitments to staff that may have been loyal; it protects the company's reputation as an employer; and it sends the right signals to the remaining employees. Research has shown that this has an important positive effect on employees who see former colleagues lose their jobs.

As a result many companies use external specialists to support them in managing the redundancy of larger groups of people, and of the most senior individuals. In cross-border acquisitions it is essential to have access to reliable legal counsel, because the costs and operational implications of getting things wrong are considerable. Even in the UK, the Transfer of Undertakings (Protection of Employment) Regulations are complex, and require careful interpretation.

Restructuring should aim to promote new and constructive employee relations. But that takes time, patience and a consistent approach.

10. Summary

There is every chance of success – but not always!

10 Summary

Successful restructuring depends on applying a selected set of actions in a particular set of circumstances. So no two situations are the same. There are common themes:

- good planning and analysis
- maintaining the right tempo
- communicating well
- establishing strong managerial controls
- responding promptly to changing conditions
- 'keeping an eye on the commercial ball.'

It also helps to have good managers who can force the pace and get things done. But perhaps most important is to have a clear picture of why you are doing it in the first place – what's wrong now, where you would like the business to go, and what it should look like when it gets there. If all of this can be represented numerically, so much the better.

Some senior managers find it difficult to resist the temptation to restructure on taking up a new appointment, or perhaps they just become bored or want to enhance their reputation. This should be avoided. There must always be a clear rationale for action with a well-argued business case, otherwise the results are likely to be disappointing.

Despite the well known horror stories, many attempts to restructure businesses are highly beneficial, producing step changes in performance, increasing shareholder value and strengthening the business' ability to cope with new challenges. Choosing the right time to act and having realistic goals are likely to lead to success.

11. Collinson Grant

11 Collinson Grant

Collinson Grant is a management consultancy. We help firms all over Europe and worldwide to restructure, merge acquisitions, cut costs, boost performance and profit, and manage people. This builds long-term relationships. We have kept some clients for over thirty years.

Our emphasis is on results and value for money. We expect to give a first class return on the investment in us. So we do not recommend action unless we are sure that the outcome will be worth it. We are not afraid to give bad news, or to champion ideas that may not be welcome.

Skills – the sort of work we do

Most of our work is on three themes – organisation, costs, and people. We use this simple framework to manage complex assignments – often with an international dimension – and to support managers on smaller, more focused projects. We help them to:

- restructure and integrate – following acquisitions or to improve profits
- rationalise the supply chain – we examine every process and interface to improve efficiency and service
- set up financial and managerial controls – we create robust systems to improve decision-making and reduce risks
- introduce Lean manufacturing and refine business processes – we analyse and improve how work is done, and use new ways to create change and make it stick
- cut costs – we make systematic analyses of overheads, direct costs and the profitability of customers and products; this helps managers to understand complexity, and to take firm steps to reduce it
- manage people – we draw up pay schemes and put them into effect, guide managers on employee relations and employment law, get better performance from people, and manage redundancy.

Our staff are seasoned consultants who have held responsible executive line positions. We work in many different sectors for large private and public companies and also in the public sector.

The roles we have played in restructuring projects include working with managers to:

- complete operational and market due diligence
- plan the post-acquisition strategy for growth
- integrate and transform operations
- improve profit and turn around failing companies
- reduce costs
- change the organisational structure
- recruit new staff and/or manage redundancies
- act as transitional managers.

Our approach and consulting style is grounded in pragmatism, urgency, value for money and objectivity. Programmes are customised to the requirement. Documentation is what is necessary to the case.

Notes on quotations

Notes on quotations

Our readers continue to enjoy the selective quotations that pepper our publications. But sometimes their origin is not quite clear, so here are some brief introductions.

Page reference   **'Famous person'**

1   **Jack Welch Jnr**, a native of Salem Massachusetts, served as Chairman and Chief Executive Officer of General Electric from 1981 to 2001. During his twenty years of leadership, Welch increased the value of the company from $13 billion to several hundred billion. His best-selling autobiography was called Jack: Straight from the Gut.

5, 82   **Albert Einstein** (1879–1955) Most people know what he looked like, but few understand what he did. Einstein's work on relativity, gravitation and radiation led to a Nobel prize and inspired many of the technological advances of the 20th century. Despite recent events underneath the Italian Dolomites, his belief in the absolute speed of light remains unchallenged.

20   **Charles Dickens** (1812–1870) Author of some of the best-loved novels in English literature and also a chronicler of the social upheaval of the Victorian age. A true 'celebrity' before the phrase had been coined – he exposed chronic poverty, the excesses of the law, political corruption and the absurdities of social conventions.

32   **Mark Twain** (1835–1910) was the pen name of Samuel Langhorne Clemens, a respected American author and humorist. He was born in Florida when Halley's Comet was visible and predicted that he would 'go out with it' as well, which he did, missing the comet's subsequent return by one day.

37   The fifteenth child of a farmer/blacksmith from Northamptonshire, England, **Benjamin Franklin** (1706–1790) rose to become one of the 'Founding Fathers of the United States'. Listed in Wikipedia as a 'political theorist, politician, postmaster, scientist, musician, inventor, satirist, civic activist, statesman and diplomat', he was obviously a very fine fellow indeed.

40	**Marcus Tullius Cicero** (106 BCE–43 BCE) was a Roman philosopher, lawyer and politician. He is widely considered to be one of Rome's greatest orators. Read Robert Harris's interesting novel Imperium to find out more.
43	**John Kennedy (JFK)** (1917–1961) A man of his time. He survived the Cuban missile crisis but not an open-top drive through Dallas. The 35th President of the United States, JFK was well regarded at the time but now nobody is quite sure why.
49	**Samuel Johnson** (1709–1784) Oft-quoted biographer, poet and lexicographer. His Dictionary of the English Language (1755), the standard reference for over a century, has since been described by Blackadder as 'the most pointless book since How to Learn French was translated into French'.
53	Author of The Affluent Society and other influential books, **J K Galbraith** (1908–2006), the celebrated American academic and economist, ridiculed the conventional wisdom that free market economics would bring benefits to all as 'the horse-and-sparrow theory: If you feed the horse enough oats, some will pass through to the road for the sparrows'.
56, 114	**Confucius** (551 BCE–479 BCE) was a revered Chinese politician, teacher and philosopher who espoused 'traditional' values of family loyalty and respect. He is credited with having written many classic texts but, as often seems the case, the scholars are now not quite so sure.
61	**Henry David Thoreau** (1817–1862) A prolific writer on diverse subjects, Thoreau was born in Massachusetts and educated at Harvard University. He was well known for his strong views on the abolition of slavery, but he also wrote passionately on how to improve (or perhaps abolish) civil government.
71	**Sherlock Holmes** (first graced the page in 1887) Notably the good friend of Dr Watson, Sherlock Holmes has transcended the written page and become perhaps the most famous fictional detective in the Western world. Not so sure about the hotel though.

73	**Peter Drucker** (1909–2005) Deserved the title 'the father of modern management' better than some other recipients. Among insights admired but insufficiently adopted is: 'The productivity of work is not the responsibility of the worker but of the manager.'
76	**Michael Hammer** (1948–2008) An American engineer, management author and a former professor of computer science at the Massachusetts Institute of Technology (MIT), famed as one of the founders of the managerial approach called business process re-engineering.
85	**Steve Jobs** (1955–2011) The fairly recently deceased co-founder of Apple Inc. currently enjoys almost legendary status as the person who brought well-designed products to eager consumers and in so doing created one of the largest businesses in the world.
94	**Aesop** is thought to have been a slave living in Greece around the 6th century BCE. He is credited with the eponymous Aesop's Fables. Although no direct evidence of their provenance has survived, they remain popular to this day – with readers young and old.
108	**Francis Bacon** died in 1626 by contracting pneumonia while studying the effects of freezing on the preservation of meat. Born in 1561, Bacon was an English philosopher, statesman, scientist, jurist and author. He served both as Attorney General and Lord Chancellor of England. Although his political career ended in disgrace, he remained extremely influential through his works, especially as philosophical advocate and practitioner of the scientific method during the scientific revolution.
112	**Bertrand Russell** (1872–1970) A Nobel laureate, Russell came from a prominent aristocratic family. He was a distinguished philosopher, particularly noted for his work on logic. Sometimes better known to the 'common man' as a leading campaigner for nuclear disarmament, he opposed the Vietnam War vigorously and was imprisoned during the First World War for his pacifism.